Serving
with Eyes
Wide Open

UPDATED EDITION

Serving with Eyes Wide Open

DOING SHORT-TERM MISSIONS
WITH CULTURAL INTELLIGENCE

David A. Livermore

BakerBooks

a division of Baker Publishing Group
Grand Rapids, Michigan

© 2006, 2013 by David A. Livermore

Published by Baker Books
a division of Baker Publishing Group
P.O. Box 6287, Grand Rapids, MI 49516-6287
www.bakerbooks.com

Printed in the United States of America

Library of Congress Cataloging-in-Publication Data
Livermore, David A., 1967–
    Serving with eyes wide open : doing short-term missions with cultural intelligence / David A. Livermore. — Updated ed.
      p. cm.
    Includes bibliographical references.
    ISBN 978-0-8010-1519-9 (pbk.)
    1. Short-term missions. 2. Cultural intelligence. I. Title.
BV2082.S56L59 2013
266′.02373—dc23   2012028377

The internet addresses, email addresses, and phone numbers in this book are accurate at the time of publication. They are provided as a resource. Baker Publishing Group does not endorse them or vouch for their content or permanence.

13   14   15   16   17   18   19   7   6   5   4   3   2   1

Contents

Foreword

I've had the privilege of knowing about Dave Livermore and observing his dedication to cross-cultural ministry for more than a decade. As with many of the early devotees of short-term missions, especially trips involving young people, Dave's interest in and commitment to short-term missions started with a view that focused primarily on giving Western Christians a great cross-cultural experience to foster their own growth.

In the late twentieth century, churches across America (and other wealthier nations) jumped at this unprecedented opportunity created by the advent of long-haul travel to go, minister, and learn in a fascinating world of cultures and adventures. Short-term missions morphed from a primary avenue for missionary recruitment to a foundational way to provoke spiritual growth in the lives of the participants.

Thankfully, Dave did not stay locked in this "missions for the benefit of me" mind-set. His long-term dedication to listening to and learning from brothers and sisters in the non-Western world transformed his perspective into what is now a commitment to genuine cross-cultural relationships and effective partnerships with the church in the majority world.

I finally met Dave personally when he was well into this journey, and I deeply appreciated his willingness to be self-critical, to ask tough questions about some of our culturally insensitive assumptions, and to practice what he preaches in this book. He has slowed down, put his passport on the shelf for a while, and asked questions about rethinking and reworking short-term missions.

This book is the result of his reflection and research. It will serve well any leader who is willing to ask questions about how short-term missions can best serve the global advancement of Christ's kingdom—and not just the experiential advancement of Christians who are wealthy enough to participate in global adventures.

Dave's global overviews, careful research, and practical tools combine his skills as a youth worker, missiologist, and anthropologist. Like a news reporter in the helicopter above the highway, Dave gives us the "skyway patrol" view of short-term missions. While we are celebrating the sheer volume of short-term missions traffic, Dave takes time to give us a sense of the road ahead. He warns us of the culturally insensitive potholes that could keep us from joining the mainstream of God's activity in the majority world. He gives voice to non-Western leaders so that we don't continue on the road to ineffectiveness. And he points us in a direction that will keep us from taking the wrong exit, a detour into our own cultural self-absorption caused by our failure to evaluate our basic assumptions and listen to our non-Western co-travelers.

Like Dave, I believe in short-term missions, and I encourage churches and ministries to get involved. But I also believe that our Western approach to short-term missions, behavior in relating to those from other cultures, and perspective on the purposes of short-term missions desperately need an overhaul and a reevaluation. *Serving with Eyes Wide Open: Doing Short-Term Missions with Cultural Intelligence* provokes this overhaul. Any leader who is willing to take time to reflect on where short-term missions fits in our Western contribution to global Christianity will find this book an essential resource.

Paul Borthwick, Development Associates International,
author of *A Mind for Missions*

Preface

Since the first edition of this book was released in 2006, I've sometimes been approached at Christian conferences by someone who says, "Hey—you're the guy who hates short-term missions, aren't you?"

It's not exactly the way I want to be known. And it's not really true. I don't hate short-term missions. But I understand why some have heard my critiques about short-term missions without also hearing me say that I think there's tremendous potential in short-term missions done well.

But what has surprised me far more is the way this book has been generously received by so many people. Many readers have said things like, "These were things I always wondered about but never really voiced." Or "This doesn't apply only to a short-term missions trip. I see the same things in how we interact with culturally diverse people at home."

Here's the deal. I don't hate short-term missions. I've been participating in short-term missions for more than twenty-five years—as a participant, a leader, and a researcher. And even to this day, I travel overseas several times a year to minister and teach in various places around the world. It's because I think short-term missions *can* be such a transformative experience for everyone involved that I've been motivated to examine the good and the bad of our North American endeavors.

The second edition of *Serving with Eyes Wide Open* includes the core of what was in the first edition: a wide-angled look at the realities of our twenty-first-century world, a focus on some conflicts between how many North Americans describe their short-term missions experiences and the perspective of the locals who receive them, and an introduction to cultural intelligence as a way to improve the ways we learn and serve.

The second edition also includes many additions and changes from the first one. I've updated the statistics and research as needed. And I've incorporated some of the things I've learned from additional reflection and interaction with people about this topic.

On the whole, I'm encouraged by the direction short-term missions is moving. Growing numbers of groups are working hard to develop reciprocal, honoring relationships with the communities and churches they visit. Orientation and even debrief sessions have come a long way. And there's a spirit driving the short-term missions movement that appears much more thoughtful than what I observed when I first began researching and talking about this fascinating phenomenon in the contemporary church.

We still have much more we can do. Not all groups are equal. There are compelling, missiologically sound pictures of short-term missions happening in countless churches and organizations. And there are still plenty of appalling examples of seemingly thoughtless, adventure-seeking groups.

I invite you to join with me in taking a careful look at the world in which we live and zooming in on how short-term missions can be a part of what God is doing for such a time as this.

Acknowledgments

First and foremost, I'm grateful to my friends scattered in places around the world who have confided in me the joys and challenges of interacting with the North American church, including me. One of my driving agendas in this book is to allow more North Americans to hear their voices.

Second, I'm grateful for the benefit of many conversations with readers of the first edition of this book. Your input provoked me to think deeper and at times differently about certain aspects of short-term missions. A growing number of researchers are now investigating this topic, and several ministry leaders are rising to the challenge to do short-term missions with cultural intelligence. It's one thing to write about these ideas. It's another thing to do something about it. Thank you to those who are actually improving short-term missions.

I have immense gratitude for my editor and friend, Bob Hosack, who took a chance on me a few years ago as an unproven author because of his shared interest in these concerns. He and the rest of the team at Baker continue to be wonderful publishing partners.

Most of all, I'm grateful for my precious daughters, Emily and Grace, and my soul mate and wife, Linda. Not only do they give me the space, inspiration, and encouragement to write, but they also embrace these ideals with me. I'm not worthy of you dear women!

Introduction

On a cool November evening in London, I was roaming the winding streets of Piccadilly Circus with my African friend Mark. This was Mark's first trip out of Africa. Experiencing the multisensory experience of the night scene in Piccadilly Circus with him is a memory I'll never forget. It was the perfect way to view a culture—Mark and I each coming from unique cultural vantage points. I'll also never forget our conversation that evening. We had just finished dinner and an orientation meeting with a group of American[1] youth pastors who had just arrived in Europe for a two-week tour during which they would conduct youth ministry training in several churches across Europe.

Mark said, "Dave, that group was just so American!"

"Wait a minute. You're talking to a full-blooded American!" I replied.

For the time being, he assured me, I was exempt from his tirade. "They didn't ask me a single question all night long," he continued. "They were loud and brash. And they have prepared for this trip just enough to make them dangerous."

Mark's first two accusations were nothing new to me. I had observed and heard those criticisms all too often about my culture. However, his concern about preparation making them dangerous intrigued me. I've spent the last several years moving in and out of many different cultures. I've participated in and led dozens of short-term missions trips, and I've always made preparation and orientation nonnegotiable. Still, was Mark onto something? Could preparation actually *hinder* one's ability to be effective cross-culturally?

Cross-cultural encounters used to be reserved for an elite set of jet-setters who traversed the international date line like the rest of us moved from one county to the next. Today, however, cross-border interactions are an everyday part of our lives. The American pastors who joined us in London are among millions of North Americans who participate in short-term missions trips each year. Some estimate that as many as four million Americans take short-term missions trips out of the country annually, and North American churches now spend as much on short-term missions trips as on long-term missionaries.[2]

Add to the ever-growing mission trip industry the business travelers who hop between Montreal, London, Beijing, and Sydney all in a matter of days. International travel is at an all-time high. And you don't even have to travel outside your own town to encounter the phenomenon of people living on opposite sides of the world but linked in ways previously unimaginable. Sitting at home in St. Louis, you can play chess on the internet with someone in China.

Even in sleepy, Midwest cities like Grand Rapids, Michigan, where I live, cross-cultural encounters abound. Just this morning I stopped at the grocery store, where a Sudanese man who arrived here a few months ago bagged my items. A couple hours later, I made a phone call to my credit-card company and ended up being routed to a call center in New Delhi, India. At lunch I overheard the couple behind me at the restaurant talking about their trip to Capetown, South Africa, next week. When I returned to my office, I opened the internet browser on my computer. It defaults to BBC News, so I was immediately viewing images from Gaza, North Korea, England, Libya, and more—all accompanied by current updates! I have more up-to-date information on what's happening in Libya right now than on how my girls are doing at school today. Cross-cultural encounters are all around us.

Neither my parents nor my in-laws have ever had a passport. I don't expect they ever will. However, my girls are on their third editions. The vast majority of the students at the universities where I teach not only have passports but also have multiple stamps throughout them.

We've never had greater accessibility and opportunity to cross over cultural lines, whether in our own backyards or twelve time zones away. We're traveling as never before.

Sadly, however, our increased accessibility to the globe doesn't seem to have dwindled our colonialist[3] tendencies. Much of the way we interact cross-culturally continues to be filled with an "our way is best" mentality. An awareness of the importance of cross-cultural sensitivity is certainly greater than a couple decades ago. However, a subtle sense among North Americans that we have the "right" culture and thus need to "convert" others to our ways still permeates much of our cross-cultural perspective and practice—whether it's work we're doing as part of a multinational corporation, a university study-abroad program, or a mission trip.

This book is an attempt to open our eyes to existing blind spots in global missions, specifically short-term missions. I want to change the way we *see* and therefore *do* short-term missions. My own cross-cultural work has often reflected the weaknesses described in this book, so I do not write as one who embodies the perfect approach to cross-cultural interaction. However, exposure to my own neocolonialism and that of others has transformed the way I interact cross-culturally. Just as important, it's altered my perspective of myself, of others, of the world, and of my faith.

That's what I desire through this book—that we pause long enough amid our life in a global village to see what we may have missed before. I want us to question our assumptions and hear the voices of locals who have received our mission trips, consulting, and training modules. I want us to be open to the idea that our overall perspective may need altering. And after sharing some of the hard-hitting perspective about where we need to realign our efforts, I promise a more solution-oriented, hopeful approach to short-term missions in the latter portion of the book.

This book applies to anyone who wants to be more effective cross-culturally—whether in preparing you for your upcoming mission trip or tour abroad, helping you relate to an immigrant at work, or enhancing the work you do overseas as part of your job. But *Serving with Eyes Wide Open* is particularly focused on those of us who engage in short-term missions—either at home or abroad. In addition to the millions of North Americans going overseas on short-term missions trips, as many or more participate in cross-cultural projects at home in their own communities and nearby states. The material in this book applies to both international and domestic cross-cultural encounters.

The short-term missions movement has had huge buy-in from other developed nations as well, including places like the United Kingdom, Australia, South Korea, and Singapore. My own research has focused primarily on those of us from the United States, and in some cases Canada, who participate in cross-cultural mission work. However, my friends from other developed nations tell me that much of what's reported here also applies to their cross-cultural practice, though I can't begin to assume its relevance beyond my own context.

Due to the ever-growing number of people doing short-term missions work abroad, an increasing number of resources are available to assist in these endeavors. Some helpful works deal specifically with the logistics and planning of such trips. Other more technical and scholarly works take a strongly theoretical approach to intercultural practice, and still others offer a more devotional approach to short-term missions and its transformational impact on the participants. Many of these are worthwhile resources, some of which I've included in the appendix.

This book, while being informed by those other helpful resources, takes a different approach—specifically examining the perspectives and assumptions we bring into our cross-cultural practices. The biggest problems in short-term missions are not technical or administrative. The biggest challenges lie in communication, misunderstanding, personality conflict, poor leadership, and bad teamwork. All too often we try to respond to these challenges by attempting to change surface-level behaviors rather than getting at the assumptions and convictions behind our behaviors. We learn the dos and don'ts about how to act when we go somewhere, yet it seems to make little difference in how we actually interact cross-culturally. We come home with zealous descriptions of how we've changed, yet within a few weeks, our lives look pretty identical to how they looked before the trip.

Serving with Eyes Wide Open is an attempt to open our eyes and see what we might otherwise miss. It's my belief that as we do so we'll not only interact in more Christ-honoring ways but also come away with a higher degree of lasting change in us and in the communities we visit.

Another priority of this book is to give voice to local church leaders from a variety of settings around the world. These brothers and sisters are on the receiving end of our short-term missions projects. Many of them are too gracious to explicitly state some of the things that emerged in the research behind this book. It's my hope that this project is one small step forward in listening to the global church, of which the North American church is now a small minority.

Finally, this book is unique in that it applies cultural intelligence, or CQ, to short-term missions. We all understand the idea of IQ—a measurement of how intellectually smart someone is. And in more recent years, psychologists have taught us about the importance of emotional intelligence, or EQ, a measurement of how well we're in tune with the emotions of ourselves and others. CQ simply draws upon some of the same ideas and research in measuring our ability to interact effectively across cultures.[4]

There are three parts to this book. Part 1 gives a wide-angle view on our twenty-first-century world and church. We live in a global village, and awareness of the pressing issues of our village is an important springboard for a discussion about cross-cultural encounters. In addition, the largest Christian communities today are in Africa and Latin America. We must understand the changing face of Christianity if we are to appropriately see what we're joining when we engage in missions cross-culturally. "Serving with eyes wide open" begins with a widened perspective on the realities of our twenty-first-century world.

Part 2 explores the conflicting perspectives on short-term missions between North Americans and the global church. It examines the assumptions that drive a great deal of our cross-cultural work. The primary source of the information in these chapters is my original research on short-term missions. For example, I studied the practice of North American pastors who went overseas for ten days to two weeks to train national pastors. The research compared the North American pastors' assessment of their cross-cultural training efforts with that of the local pastors who received the training. This, combined with research on short-term missions by others and me, and the literature of cross-cultural interactions as a whole, led to the six areas of conflicting perspectives described in part 2. These realities permeate the assumptions of our short-term work.

Part 3 provides a framework for applying CQ to short-term missions. The material in this section helps us apply our widened perspective and actually *do* short-term missions more effectively. We don't have to try to master CQ before our next trip. Instead, we want to embark on a lifelong journey of using CQ to more effectively love God and love others—on our short-term missions trips and in our everyday lives back home.

It's an amazing privilege to interact with people from other cultures. The seven billion people around the world are so much like us yet very different. May this book enhance the way we reflect God's glory when encountering the diverse people with whom we share the world. We will grapple with some hard-hitting realities in the pages that follow, but I encourage you to persevere; that's not the end of the story. I have great hope for the opportunities that lie on the horizon as we increasingly become part of a transient, global church traveling from everywhere to everywhere. Open your eyes. There's much to see in the movement of short-term missions and, more importantly, the movement of God in the world at large. Thanks for embarking on this journey with me.

PART I

Looking through a Wide-Angle Lens

Globalization and the Church

We begin broadening our view by looking through a wide-angle lens at the twenty-first-century world. After surviving the Cold War, the nuclear arms race, two world wars, several genocide attempts, and numerous totalitarian regimes, we find ourselves well into a new century. North Americans in 1900 had a life expectancy of forty-seven, whereas today it's seventy-six. Our world has undergone immense change over the last century. The Christian church has been in a state of major transition as well—both local congregations and the church at large.

Widening our perspective on our world should be an ongoing process for all of us. The next two chapters present a few snapshots of our world—the world as a whole and the worldwide Christian church. Like any snapshot, these pictures give us only a glimpse into the realities behind the images. It's important to begin with a wide-angle view before focusing more specifically on short-term missions work. Join me on a quick tour around the world as we begin the journey toward serving with eyes wide open.

1

One World

Snapshots of the Globe

On a recent visit to Seattle, I met my friend Tony for lunch. Tony lives in Mexico City, and we were both visiting Seattle at the same time. We met at an easy-to-find spot in Seattle's Chinatown and walked through the international district for a few minutes before ending up at a French café. We walked inside, and soon after we were seated, a Haitian woman came up to take our order. She suggested some English Breakfast tea with our entrées. As she took our order, a group of Japanese businessmen sat down at the table behind us. I looked at Tony and said, "Do you see what just happened? In a matter of three minutes, we've encountered Mexican, American, Chinese, French, Haitian, English, and Japanese cultures!" Tony and I launched into an interesting discussion about our globalized world. Experiencing a mosaic of cultures as Tony and I did that day used to be reserved for the jet-setting few who hung out in international airports. But the world is becoming increasingly smaller for all of us.

At the same time, Americans still fare poorly in our awareness of what's going on in the world. Our collective global consciousness is pretty dismal, and many mainstream media outlets do little to help. Our family often hosts international guests in our home, and they're forever frustrated that they can't get more than a passing glimpse of world events from our major news shows. Becoming globally conscious doesn't come easily. It requires extra effort on our part.

We're all citizens of a global world, whether we realize it or not. Our journey into a widened perspective on global missions begins by looking at some of the predominant issues facing our twenty-first-century world. While by no means an exhaustive list, some of the most important issues facing us include the following snapshots.

Snapshot 1: Growing Population of the World

Every second, four babies are born. Four more babies were just born . . . and four more . . . and four more . . . and four more. It continues day after day after day, the population of the world growing at a rapid rate. More than twice as many people are born each day than die. All this adds up to a world population of more than seven billion people. Line us all up in single file around the world and we'd circle the globe more than 112 times. At this rate, we can expect a population of eight billion people by the year 2025.[1]

Where do all these people live? Twenty percent live in China. Twenty percent live in India. Five percent live in the United States. Fifty-five percent live in the other nations of the world. Developing nations are growing rapidly while their industrialized neighbors remain relatively static. The seven billion of us are scattered throughout approximately two hundred nations, but there are more than five thousand identifiable ethnocultural groups in the world.[2]

Nearly half of the people in the world are children. Forty percent of the world's population is under the age of fifteen, while less than 20 percent of North Americans are under fifteen. Many of our global children have a dismal future. It's hard to grow up when you're poor, marginalized, and forgotten. Health services are few and far between for most children in the world.

My wife, Linda, and I have often struggled with whether our girls' school system, teachers, and the corresponding curricula are our best options for them. Meanwhile, over one billion children have *no* options and *no* access to schools. The majority of schools that do exist in the world are poorly run and costly to attend.

Perspective. That's what we're after in this journey together. Open your eyes. Wider. Look around you. There have never been this many people alive in the world. Four more babies were just born, and four more . . .

Snapshot 2: Poverty versus Wealth

Many of our fellow citizens around the globe face desperate economic circumstances. This is a perspective I've continually tried to give my kids. One time shortly after dinner, Grace, who was five or six at the time, said, "Daddy, I'm hungry. I need a snack." Emily, her older sister, smirked at me, knowing this was the perfect opportunity for my soapbox speech. Right on cue I started in. "Gracie, how can you be hungry? We just finished a good dinner. Millions of children in the world won't get a meal like that all month—"

"Sorry, Daddy," Grace interrupted. "I mean, I *want* a snack."

This has become standing practice for us as a family. Whenever one of us says, "I need . . ." someone else chimes in and says, "Need or want?" My girls love it when they catch me saying, "I *need* coffee." We're working hard to remember that we're among the "haves" when so many in the world are among the "have nots." The point is not to be guilt-ridden, middle-class Christians. But we want to live with a spirit of generosity and be continually mindful of the chasm between the rich and the poor in our world. Read these statistics slowly and deliberately:

- Twenty percent of the people in the world live on one dollar a day.
- Another 20 percent live on two dollars a day.
- Twenty percent of us live on more than seventy dollars a day.
- The remaining 40 percent are somewhere in between. [3]

And how about this? The combined income of the 447 wealthiest people in the world is larger than the combined income of 50 percent of the world's population. Did you catch that? Four hundred and forty-seven people have more money than the combined assets of 3.5 billion people in the world![4]

Sisay, a character in Richard Dooling's riveting novel *White Man's Grave*, is a North American who has moved to Sierra Leone, where he has become fully immersed as a local. After five years away from the United States, Sisay describes the sickening experience he had going back for a brief visit to the United States:

> I resolved to sit on my mother's front porch and soak up some American village life to remind myself of what I had left behind. It was Saturday. My mother's next-door neighbor, a well-groomed, weight-gifted, vertically challenged accountant named Dave, brought out a leaf blower, a lawn mower, a leaf grinder, a mulcher, an edger, and a weed trimmer. He worked all day, making a terrific racket, chopping, trimming, and spraying toxins on a small patch of ground, which produced absolutely no food, only grass. *The rest of the world spent the day standing in swamp water trying to grow a few mouthfuls of rice, while Dave sat on his porch with a cold beer admiring his chemical lawn.* Sickening? You bet. It was time to go back to Africa.[5]

This is more than well-written fiction; this is reality. Americans make up 5 percent of the world's population, but we consume 50 percent of the world's resources. Think about that. We consume half of the world's resources. The problem of hunger in the world is *not* the earth's inability to produce food for seven billion people; it's the inequitable distribution of food.

Ravi, a seven-year-old boy I met in Delhi, is among the 95 percent of the world's population that isn't American. Ravi works ten to twelve hours a day, seven days a week, shining shoes on the streets of Delhi. Ravi faces four years of bonded labor in order to pay back a thirty-five-dollar loan his parents took out for his sister's wedding. Ravi will spend the next four years paying off a debt that's less than what I spent on dinner out last night. The inequities continue:

- More than two billion children live in our world, half in poverty.
- One of every four children in the world has to work instead of going to school.
- Eight percent of people in the world own a car.

Perspective. Perspective on "need." Perspective on "hunger." Perspective on "money." Do you feel as if you're living paycheck to paycheck? You may well be, and my point is not to diminish the financial challenges facing many North Americans. But it's all about perspective. It's all about serving with eyes wide open.

Snapshot 3: Disease

If the above statistics are not enough to ruin your appetite, how about this? Thirty thousand people will die today from *preventable* diseases. More than three thousand Americans lost their lives on 9/11. Many of us remember where we were when we first heard the news that day. Three thousand lives were lost in a matter of hours. We pause each year on September 11 to remember the victims and their families, and we should.

Yet how many of us will remember where we were when we learned that thirty thousand people will die today from preventable diseases? It's all too easy to read that, say, "Wow! That's horrible," and move on. Thirty thousand people will die today. More than two hundred thousand, the population of the city where I live, will die this week from preventable diseases.

A great many of the deaths today will occur because the victims couldn't get basic medicines that I can buy over the counter at a local drug store. Many of those who die today will be children. In fact, a child dies of hunger every sixteen seconds. Just about every time I take a breath, another child dies of hunger.

- Forty percent of the people in the world lack basic sanitation facilities.
- Over one billion people have unsafe drinking water.[6]

Perspective. Perspective on the world in which we live. That's where we're headed with all this.

One of the worst diseases facing us is HIV/AIDS. AIDS threatens the social well-being of entire nations. Almost forty million people are infected with the virus, with another one hundred thousand infected daily. These numbers are expected to double by 2015.

We must dispel the notion that AIDS is simply just punishment upon those who are sexually promiscuous. The number one way children in Mozambique contract the HIV virus is by sharpening their pencils with their fathers' razor blades.[7]

In many parts of sub-Saharan Africa, the pastorate has become a "burial business." Pastors bury AIDS victims daily, while teenagers and grandparents figure out how to lead households in which both parents have died. Over fifteen million children under the age of fifteen have lost one or both parents to AIDS, and that figure is expected to double by the year 2015.[8]

The next wave of the pandemic is expected to be in India, China, and Russia, home to almost one-third of the world's population. We are at the *beginning* of this crisis, not the end. This is a century-long struggle.

Of the seven billion people in the world, 40 percent live on two dollars or less a day. AIDS is eliminating entire generations in some communities. All the numbers can become overwhelming—even numbing—but we must gain perspective on the world in which we live. Let's open our eyes in order to improve the way we serve.

Snapshot 4: Refugees

Too many people on our planet are being forced out of their homes and communities. There's been a dramatic increase in the number of refugees over the last thirty years. In 1975, 2.5 million people were known to be refugees. Today more than 12 million people have been forced out of their native countries. Another 24 million people have fled conflict and persecution and are internally displaced within their own countries. The vast majority of refugees are women and children, and more than 65 percent are Muslim.[9]

As if being displaced from their homes and communities isn't enough, militia groups, rebels, and government leaders often take advantage of vulnerable refugees. Aid sent to refugees is often intercepted and horded by abusive leaders. Drugs intended to heal children are taken and sold, and food sent to families is enjoyed by warlords. Worst of all, refugees are abused physically and often killed simply to make a statement to other groups struggling for power.[10]

Sadly, young mothers such as Isatu Turay in Sierra Leone are not an anomaly in the twenty-first century. Isatu and her husband were living in a refugee camp in Sierra Leone along with their four young children. One morning heavily armed men entered their house and demanded all their possessions. The rebels became upset when Isatu and her husband had only thirty thousand *leones* (local currency) to give them. On the spot the rebels killed Isatu's younger sister, who was also living there, and brutally murdered Isatu's husband right before her eyes.

Isatu gathered her children and fled from the refugee camp into the bush, where she ran into another group of rebels who were lining people up and chopping off their hands. Isatu says, "I was praying heavily, and then my two-year-old daughter started to cry. They said the child was causing lots of noise for them. One of them took her from me while another dug a hole to bury her alive. I could not do anything, and my baby cried until she died."[11]

Isatu's story speaks for itself. *Perspective.*

Snapshot 5: McWorld

Globalization is a broad term with many meanings, but the term is most often associated with the expansion of business and capitalism across national borders. Serving with eyes wide open includes gaining perspective on this growing reality in our world. Marketing products and services that have been profitable in developed nations and selling them overseas is often referred to as the McDonaldization of the world, or McWorld for short.

McDonald's is the epitome of McWorld. You can get the same french fries in Quito, Delhi, and Toronto. And the most universal product in the world is Coca-Cola. Or consider one of my addictions—Starbucks! You could be dropped into a Starbucks in Bangkok and have a hard time knowing whether you're in Bangkok, Seattle, Shanghai, or Sydney. The same drinks are available; the same font adorns the signage; and the chairs, lighting, color on the walls, and music are all strangely familiar. It's all part of the McWorld experience of Starbucks. Granted, even McDonald's, KFC, and Starbucks have some menu offerings that reflect local tastes and customs. But on the whole, the experience at a McWorld business is much the same wherever you go.

When I travel, I love to eat in local establishments, and I thoroughly enjoy trying new foods. I have to admit, however, that sometimes I'm really happy to find a Starbucks where I can get my predictable, favorite drink. Yet I'm sometimes haunted by the implications of getting Indonesians to switch from tea to Frappuccinos, from sandals to Nikes, from oxen to SUVs, and from indigenous movies to Hollywood. This tension needs to be incorporated into our widened perspective on the twenty-first-century world.

For example, consider that on average North American companies make a 42-percent return on their China operations. Apparel workers in the United States make $9.56 an hour. In El Salvador, apparel workers make $1.65. In China, they make between 68 and 88 cents.[12] Christian businesspeople need to help us wrestle with these realities and consider the ethical issues involved and the accountability structures needed for individuals and organizations working cross-culturally.

There's a growing movement in the corporate arena described as "conscious capitalism." I'm excited about business professionals looking holistically at how to use business to respond to some of the pressing issues of our world. And I appreciate the economists and business leaders who are helping us grapple with the complexities of McWorld rather than simply saying it's all good or it's all bad. The realities of McWorld need to be included in our widened perspective.

In addition, McWorld is creating a virtual, global culture of sorts, especially among youth. A few years ago, a New York City–based ad agency videotaped rooms of teenagers in twenty-five different countries. The convergence of what was found in rooms from Los Angeles to Mexico City to Tokyo made it difficult to see any cultural differences. Basketballs sat next to soccer balls, and closets overflowed with an international, unisex uniform—baggy Levis or Diesel jeans, NBA jackets, and rugged shoes from Timberland or Dr. Martens. "In a world divided by trade wars and tribalism, teenagers, of all people, are the new unifying force. From the steamy playgrounds of Los Angeles to the stately boulevards of Singapore, kids show amazing similarities in taste, language, and attitude. . . . Propelled by mighty couriers like MTV, trends spread with sorceress speed. . . .

Teens almost everywhere buy a common gallery of products: Reebok sports shoes, Procter & Gamble Cover Girl makeup, Sega and Nintendo video games, Pepsi, etc."[13]

We must not too quickly assume that globalization implies we're moving toward a uniform, global culture. Cultural differences abound, and we'll see that throughout this book. However, to a certain degree, globalization is shaping the lives of individuals from the urban centers of Shanghai to the remote villages of Madagascar.

McWorld has brought cross-cultural encounters into our daily lives. Working alongside refugees from Bosnia and Sudan, instant messaging people with similar interests across twenty-four time zones, and working in organizations that assume a global presence are just a few ways we encounter globalization.

Snapshot 6: Fundamentalism versus Pluralism

While seemingly more philosophical, this last snapshot is as important to our perspective on the world as the others. On the one hand, there is a growing movement of fundamentalists in today's world who declare, "There is *one* right way to view the world, and it's our way." Simultaneously, a growing number of pluralists say, "There's *no* one right way to view the world. Develop your own view. Just don't force it on me."

The clash of fundamentalism versus pluralism is at the center of most of our contemporary conflicts and wars. A world coming together culturally and commercially is simultaneously becoming more and more divided religiously and ethnically. In the 1990s, words like *jihad* and *al-Qaeda* were unfamiliar to most North Americans. Now they're part of our everyday vocabulary. Watching news reports of fourteen-year-old boys in Afghanistan skipping along with AK-47s strapped over their shoulders has almost become ho-hum to us. Yet many Americans are still confused as to why the terrorists hate us so much. In relation to suicide bombers, we ask, "What's wrong with those people that they'd kill themselves in order to dominate innocent people?"

If anyone should understand the conviction and passion driving the terrorist movements around the world, it's Christians. Jihad, in its mildest form, is a kind of Islamic zeal held by people committed to proselytizing the world no matter what it takes. Of course, it becomes extreme when it gets expressed through bloody holy war on behalf of religious conviction—just as the Crusades were a case of "Christian evangelism gone bad." As a concept, however, fundamentalist fervor is as familiar to Christians, Hindus, Arabs, and Germans as it is to Muslims.[14] Jihad, an Islamic expression of fundamentalism, is simply the absolute confidence in the truth of one's position.

In contrast, pluralism attempts to eliminate the dominance of any one religion or viewpoint. It assumes that multiple and conflicting opinions and philosophies should exist and, further, should be regarded as equals. This kind of pluralistic philosophy permeates the story lines of movies, songs, and books distributed through globalization. Globalization is typically seen as an expression and agent of pluralism. Yet globalization also seems to be based on an essential value held by radical fundamentalists—the core value of domination. Bringing the world a uniform offering of products, services, and entertainment options is assumed to be good for all.

The coexistence of passionate pluralists with ruthless fundamentalists will continue to create tensions worthy of our attention. Such tension is faced by the worldwide community of Christians as well. Lamin Sanneh, a Gambian Christian scholar, says, "Northern, liberal Christianity has become a 'do-as-you-please' religion, deeply accommodated to the post-Christian values of the secular northlands. The new Christianity of the global south and east [e.g., Africa, Latin America, India], which bears the scars of hardship and persecution, will clash increasingly with its urbane and worldly northern counterpart."[15] We'll further explore the realities of the Christian church in the twenty-first century in the next chapter.

Concluding Thoughts

These snapshots are an initial step toward helping us open our eyes. The statistics, inequities, and sheer enormity of global issues facing our generation can be mind-numbing. What can I possibly do about the fact that one in thirty-seven hundred American women die in childbirth, whereas one in sixteen sub-Saharan African women die in childbirth?

I'm not interested in putting you on an overwhelming guilt trip. Guilt and shame do little to change these realities. But I do want to bring perspective to how we live our lives and think about the circumstances of many of the people we'll encounter on our short-term missions experiences. Perspective and awareness alone are not enough. But they are an essential starting point for serving with eyes wide open.

2

One Church

The Changing Face of Christianity

Picture the typical Christian. What do you see? Perhaps you think of the people in your small group Bible study or the people you pass as you walk into church. Or maybe you think of the groupies who attend every Christian conference and concert that hit town or the elderly woman who religiously reads her Bible and prays each morning. While clearly part of the body of Christ, none of them are even close to how the majority of Christians look.

The "typical" Christian in the world is better portrayed as a woman living in a village in Nigeria or in a Brazilian *flavella*. The vast majority of Christians are young, poor, theologically conservative, female, and people of color.[1] As we grow in our understanding of the changing face of Christianity, there's great potential for improving how we do short-term missions. The North American church is no longer the trendsetter and center of Christianity, though we still have a significant role. Serving with eyes wide open includes changing our assumptions about the worldwide Christian church and our part therein.

By sheer majority alone, the Western church *used* to be the trend-setter for the rest of the Christian church. In 1800, only 1 percent of Christians lived outside North America and Western Europe. In 1900, 10 percent of all Christians lived outside North America and Western Europe. By 2000, more than two-thirds of the Christian church lived outside North America and Western Europe. The center of gravity in the body of Christ has shifted southward. The largest Christian communities today are not in the US Bible Belt but in Africa and Latin America.[2]

As a reflection of this reality, from here on we'll use the term *majority world church* to refer to the church outside North America and Western Europe. This term was coined by church leaders gathered from these nations at the 2004 Lausanne Committee for World Evangelism in Pattaya, Thailand. They collaboratively rejected the terms previously used to describe them, most frequently *third world church*, a term they viewed as degrading.[3] Instead, *majority world church* is a descriptive term that refers to the church in those regions of the world where the greatest population of Christians live—outside North America and Western Europe.

Just as with the world at large, it's impossible to accurately generalize about the majority world church. However, since many of us have limited experience with anything other than the churches we attend week after week, it's helpful to pause and consider some of the common characteristics of the majority world church by looking at a few more snapshots.

Snapshot 1: Unprecedented Growth

Many contemporary sociologists are confounded by the pace at which Christianity is growing around the world. Endless predictions were made throughout the twentieth century that suggested Christianity would unravel alongside colonialism. However, "instead of Christianity fading away along with the empire, it unexpectedly grew and spread."[4] New faith communities came into being without a colonial order to maintain them, and they grew with a flavor and look different from those brought to them by the imperialists.

The pace at which the majority church is growing is phenomenal. Consider a few of the statistics:

- On average, 178,000 people convert to Christianity daily.
- In Latin America, 35,000 conversions occur each day. There were 50,000 believers reported in Latin America in 1900. By 1980, there were more than 20 million, and the number is now over 480 million.
- In China, 28,000 conversions occur daily. When China became closed to missionaries in 1950, there were reportedly one million Christians in China. Today's estimates are near 100 million.
- In Indonesia, the largest Islamic country in the world, at least one million people convert to Christianity each year.
- India has more than 85 million believers. Two hundred teams travel the nation with an Indian version of the *Jesus* film, entitled *The Man of Peace*, and report 100,000 conversions monthly!
- In 1900, Korea was deemed impossible to penetrate with the gospel. Today, South Korea is reported to be more than 40 percent Christian, with more than 7,000 Christian churches in Seoul alone.
- More people have confessed Christ in Iran in the past ten years than in the previous thousand years combined! Thriving churches are found in almost every Iranian city and village.
- Daily, 20,000 conversions occur in Africa. Forty percent of Africa is said to be Christian now.
- None of the fifty largest churches in the world are found in North America. Check out the size of a few of these congregations. In Seoul, Korea, the Yoido Full Gospel Church has 837,000 members. In Abidjan, Ivory Coast, there are 150,000 members in one congregation. Another 150,000 members attend Yotabeche Methodist Church in Santiago, Chile, and 120,000 members attend Deeper Life Bible Church in Lagos, Nigeria.[5]

Some question these statistics, and that's fair. Simply counting the number of people who say a prayer or espouse to follow Jesus is not enough. We're called to make disciples who in turn have a transformational impact on their communities. Regardless, sociologists and missiologists agree that unprecedented growth is happening in the

Christian church worldwide. Something is happening in God's people around the world. Clearly the revolution of Jesus Christ continues to transcend the many atrocities and inequities described in chapter 1.

Christianity is the fastest-growing religion in the world, with a 6.9 percent growth rate, compared to 2.7 percent for Muslims, 2.2 percent for Hindus, and 1.7 percent for Buddhists.[6] The story of Christianity represents a fundamental and historical shift in worldwide religions. Christianity is not held captive by a particular culture. In fact, more languages and cultural expressions are used in Christian liturgy, devotion, worship, and prayer than in any other religion.[7]

Add the burgeoning growth of the church to your perspective on the twenty-first-century church. Open your eyes. Those of us who are members of God's people are part of a worldwide revolution that is growing with racing speed.

Snapshot 2: Persecution? Of Course!

The phenomenal growth of the church has not come without a cost. More Christians have been martyred for their faith in this century than in the previous nineteen centuries combined. Christians in the majority world church suffer brutal persecution. For most of the majority world church, persecution is commonplace and expected. As a result, many portions of the Bible make much more immediate sense to them. The stories of Mordecai and Esther, Daniel and friends, and Paul and Silas read like their daily news.[8]

Persecution is especially prevalent for Christians living in many of the remnant communist countries, including China, North Korea, Vietnam, Cuba, and Laos. North Korea has been in "first place" for three years in a row as the least religiously free nation in the world. Religious persecution is also prevalent in parts of the Islamic world, such as Sudan, Saudi Arabia, Iran, Pakistan, Egypt, Indonesia, and Uzbekistan. These states live by a fundamentalist conviction that there is one right way to see the world: through Islam.

You won't often hear these stories from your news outlet, or even from the persecuted themselves, because for them persecution is just a fact of life when you're a Christian. Almost daily, young Christian boys are stolen from their parents in Sudan and taken to "cultural cleansing camps" where they are forcibly converted to a fundamentalist sect. They're then sold at open-air slave markets. This is happening today! Right now fellow members in the Christian church are experiencing this kind of Paul-like persecution.

Take a minute to visit Voice of the Martyr's website, www.perse cution.com, for a timely story about someone in the majority world church who is experiencing persecution today.

Snapshot 3: Communal Decision Making

Another reality in the majority world church is an emphasis on communal decision making rather than an individualist approach. I've often been involved in developing ministry partnerships between different organizations across cultures. When I do so with organizations led by North American ministry leaders, the process typically involves a few conversations with the key decision makers at the table, and the agreement is formed. Sometimes a variety of staff play a part in the decision-making process, but at the end of the day, the partnership is solidified between one or two key leaders.

The process is very different when developing partnerships with many ministries in the majority world. One reason is the commitment of majority world church leaders to a more communal decision-making process. The leaders deliberately wrestle with the implications of a decision for many groups and whether it will promote harmony. This doesn't mean decision making and leadership are approached in an egalitarian manner in which everyone has equal voice. In fact, many majority world church leaders are far more hierarchical and paternalistic than egalitarian. However, the decision-making process occurs collectively with many people rather than with a couple of key leaders making decisions in isolation.

Historian Peter Brown sees the communal nature of the majority world church as strangely reminiscent of the Christian church in the third and fourth centuries. A radical sense of community is what made Christianity so appealing to people at that time. It allowed people to move from the wide, impersonal world into a miniature community. In the same way, many Christians in the majority world today find a far greater sense of identity with their local churches than they do

with being citizens of Peru or Nigeria. Communities of faith fill the
void of disintegrated families and tribes, which have been eroded
by ethnic cleansing, disease, and famine. The intimacy experienced
among Christian faith communities in the majority world is compa-
rable to the intimacy of a large family gathering.[9]

An emphasis on community and interdependence is one way majority world pastors have adapted the tools and philosophies they received
from Western missionaries. For example, the emphasis on helping a
church become self-supporting has been a driving agenda of Western
missions over the last several decades, as expressed in the "three-self"
formula. According to the three-self formula, national churches should
be self-propagating, self-supporting, and self-governing. Three-self is an
appropriate reaction against "spoon-feeding," where national churches
remain dependent upon Western missionaries and Western funds.[10]

However, some majority world church leaders aren't convinced that
the three-self model is the right approach. They argue that the three-
self movement comes from an individualist perspective rather than
one developed for an interdependent church around the world. Isaac
Mwase, a Christian scholar with roots in Jamaica and Zimbabwe, says,
"Unless the economies of poverty in the global South change dramati-
cally in the future, Christian solidarity would seem to demand external
support. What is needed is *not* self-sufficiency among the poor, but a
way of partnering across cultural and economic differences that affirms
Christian solidarity, the interdependency of the Body of Christ."[11]

When 40 percent of the people in the world earn less than two
dollars a day and North Americans earn more than seventy dollars
a day, can there ever be a point where majority world churches support themselves exclusively? These are the kinds of issues we need to
explore with the majority world church.

The majority world church believes in interdependence and is trying to teach the Western church about it. We must figure out how to
have healthy and mutually rewarding interdependent relationships.
This plays directly into how we approach our short-term missions
efforts. Those of us on short-term missions trips usually assume we
have something to offer the churches and communities we visit, and
sometimes we do. However, we must go beyond merely saying we need
to learn from their churches as well. In truth, there is much for us to

learn from the majority world church. These snapshots are simply an attempt to help us see a few of the inspiring characteristics of the majority world church. We'll look more specifically at the implications of these snapshots for short-term missions, but initially let's continue to open our eyes to see the big picture.

Snapshot 4: Beware the "Powers"

Another key thread in the majority world church is the core belief that we live in a dynamic, spiritual universe. While an awareness of demonic forces seldom goes beyond a thriller movie for many of us, principalities and powers are conscious realities to most of our fellow Christians around the world. Much like the first-century believers in Ephesus and Colossae, people in the majority world have an extraordinary fear of hostile, supernatural powers.

The African church is especially aware of the supernatural world. Africans, whether Christian or not, believe the universe is inhabited by the devil and a host of spiritual forces. Nearly all African religions believe strongly in the existence of all kinds of evil spirits and that these spirits influence human life in many ways. "Witchcraft beliefs remain pervasive and persistent, and no amount of denial can shift that reality, at least in Christian Africa."[12]

The belief of the majority world church in supernatural and demonic powers doesn't lead these Christians to hopeless fatalism. Instead, majority world Christians are much more aware of the importance of being vigilant against the active, dangerous spirit world lurking around them. One African pastor was asked if he thinks there's a demon behind every bush, to which he replied, "There are lots more demons than there are bushes!"

The reality of the demonic world to people in the majority world church helps explain their particular interest in Paul's letters to the Ephesians and the Colossians. First-century Ephesus and Colossae cultures were inundated with sorcery, magic, and divination. This reality is demonstrated by Paul's frequent references to the "powers of darkness." There are more references to principalities and powers in Ephesians and Colossians than in any other book of the Bible. Many Western commentators have explained away Paul's multiple references to these dark forces as metaphors for the social and political structures that existed in first-century Ephesus and Colossae. Majority world church leaders, however, see these powers as literal, personal, and organized forces of evil with which they must contend on a day-to-day basis. They readily identify with Paul's words.[13]

Most North American Christians espouse belief in the existence of demons and spiritual forces, but this belief rarely moves beyond theory for us. We're intrigued by stories about demons when we hear about someone else's experience or warn kids against using a Ouija board, but our day is rarely impacted by the fear of spiritual forces lurking about. This is a key difference between our lives and those of our brothers and sisters in the majority world. This sheds light on the next snapshot too.

Snapshot 5: God's Provision Is Immediate and Direct

Believing in a dynamic universe with supernatural powers all around compels majority world Christians to pray with a greater sense of urgency and dependency. A member in a majority world church is much more likely to expect immediate and direct provision from God than a "typical" North American believer. You haven't experienced prayer until you've prayed with a group of Christians in the majority world church whose very lives are dependent upon God. Of course, every minute of our lives is dependent upon God as well. However, we have been so influenced by the comforts of life in the West that the miracles of Jesus often seem like a first-century phenomenon rather than a reality for today.

In the majority world, huge and growing Christian populations are moving toward the kind of supernaturalism embodied by Jesus and his first-century followers. This is another reason why the Bible is more easily understood by non-Western believers. Christian communities in the majority world as diverse as Protestants, evangelicals, Orthodox, and Catholics proclaim a Christianity that includes Jesus's power over the evil forces that inflict calamity and sickness upon the human race.[14]

Many of these snapshots are different angles on some of the same realities. Belief in the spirit world and day-to-day persecution are part of why the majority world church is much more aware of its daily dependence on God's provision. For example, the belief in God's immediate and direct provision is often the only coping mechanism available to majority church leaders such as Brother Yun. Yun, frequently referred to as the "heavenly man," is one of China's most persecuted house church leaders. Yun has suffered endless torture and imprisonment throughout his growing ministry in China while also reporting numerous episodes of God miraculously sustaining him.

One day after Yun was beaten and paraded through the streets for several hours, he was brought into an interrogation room where he was tightly bound, further beaten, and questioned. Despite Yun's pain and anguish, he experienced an unusual measure of confidence in God's protection over him. "Suddenly I remembered how the angels had opened the prison gates for Peter to escape. The rope that bound my arms behind my back suddenly snapped by itself! I didn't tear the ropes off, but kept them loosely in place. I decided to try to escape." As the officers attended to a phone call in the next room, Yun got up, walked through the middle of the courtyard, and leapt over an eight-foot wall. Yun says, "The God of Peter wonderfully helped me leap over the wall and escape."[15]

Yun, like most of the majority world church leaders I meet, prefers not to focus on the sensational miracles and experiences of suffering that have inundated his life. Instead, he prefers to emphasize the character and beauty of Christ, who sustains him. May God stir us from our complacency through the examples of our brothers and sisters who believe in God's direct and immediate provision.

Snapshot 6: Missionaries from Everywhere to Everywhere

One of the most exciting missions phenomena today is the Back to Jerusalem movement, a missions initiative among the Christian Chinese church. Specifically, the Back to Jerusalem movement is an initiative to proclaim the gospel and establish fellowships of believers in all the countries, cities, towns, and ethnic groups between China and Jerusalem. Along this route are the three other largest faith systems—Islam, Buddhism, and Hinduism.[16]

Back to Jerusalem is one of many missionary movements occurring in the majority world church. One morning I had breakfast with a

Filipino missionary I'll call Anna. Anna has been serving in China for five years. I asked, "Anna, how long did it take you to raise the funds to leave the Philippines and begin your work in China?"

She replied, "Oh, it was just a few weeks. I found out how much the airfare was, I told my church, and we began praying. And a few weeks later I was on the plane."

A bit puzzled, I continued, "But what about the rest of your support? How about the other funds for your living expenses once you got there?"

Her face lit up as she said, "Oh, Brother Dave, I just live by faith. God meets my every need."

Or travel to Nigeria. Several thousand Nigerians are serving as missionaries with one hundred agencies in more than fifty countries. Nigeria has long been viewed as a mission field, but now it's becoming a major missionary-sending country. For every missionary who now enters Nigeria, five Nigerians go out as missionaries to other fields of service.

Together the United States and the United Kingdom still send out the largest missions force in the world, but close behind are India, South Korea, and Brazil.[17] We're in a whole new era of missions. We are still an important player and need to continue to obediently send missionaries from the Western church. But we must realize we're joining missionaries from around the world to go to the world.

Snapshot 7: Help Wanted—Leaders!

Much more can be said about what's occurring in the majority world church, but let's look at one last snapshot for now. With the unprecedented growth of Christianity, seven thousand new church leaders are needed daily to care for the growing church. The burgeoning growth of the Christian church is creating a leadership chasm.

- Eighty-five percent of churches in the world are led by men and women who have no formal training in theology or ministry.
- If every Christian training institute in the world operated at 120 percent capacity, less than 10 percent of the unequipped leaders would be trained.

- Eight out of ten nationals who come to the West to receive training never return home.
- Leaders from every non-Western region say their number one need is leadership training.[18]

We have to be cautious about how we respond to this reality. While leaders say their number one need is leadership training, many of them don't want to use Western models to meet that need. Many residential training institutes sit empty around the world because they have been ineffective at providing the leadership training and ministry skills needed by pastors in the majority world church. In addition, majority world church leaders are intolerant of theological training that engages the head and not the heart.

We must also hold the need for leadership training in tension with the knowledge and skills many of these pastors have acquired through life experience. Brother Yun says that house pastors in China have been trained by "the foot chains that bind us and the leather whips that bruise us."[19] Through the seminary of prison, these leaders have learned many valuable lessons about God that no book or course could ever teach. This "on the job training" coupled with formal training and resources will assist these leaders as they continue to shepherd their congregations.

Ministry training for pastors is an area where interdependent models need to be developed to help meet the need. A realistic perspective on the realities of the global church has to include the huge need for equipped ministry leaders.

Concluding Thoughts

The shifting of Christianity's center to the south and the east in our world is reason to celebrate. Sometimes when North American Christians hear these snapshots, they ask, "Where have we gone wrong? Why are we suddenly becoming a minority?" Much in the Western church needs alignment. Yet despite our flawed missions efforts over the last century, God has used these very efforts to expand the church around the world. The primary reason that 70 percent of Christians live outside North America and Western Europe today is because of the unprecedented growth of Christianity from West to East.

Be inspired! God is doing amazing things through the church every-where. Our brothers and sisters all over the world provide a glimpse into how God is working. They inspire us to remain faithful. The majority world church would want you to know it's far from perfect and has many flaws of its own. That's the beauty of God's amazing ability to take our imperfect efforts and use them to reflect God's glory.

I hope you're starting to grow in your perspective of what it looks like to encounter the twenty-first-century world. The world with all its needs and disparities described in chapter 1 is a world in which God is continually calling people to salvation. The reality of Reve-lation 7:9—where people from every nation, tribe, and people group will gather to worship Jesus—has never seemed more plausible. The church exists in some form in every geopolitical nation of the world. Let us reflect on what it means to be joined together with disciples of Jesus all over the world. Open your eyes to your sister in Egypt and your brother in Chile. We need them in view as we do short-term missions.

PART 2

Conflicting Images

*The North American Perspective versus
the Majority World Church Perspective
on Short-Term Missions*

The exciting movement of God among people all over the world is exactly why short-term missions deserves our careful attention. Never before have more North American Christians had the chance to see firsthand what God is doing around the globe.

Throughout the last twenty years, short-term missions trips have become a standing part of most churches' annual calendars. Twenty-nine percent of all US adolescents participate in some kind of cross-cultural service project before graduating from high school.[1] Physicians, teachers, builders, mechanics, business leaders, families, senior citizens, and youth groups are all part of the short-term missions movement. Many travel as part of teams, and some go alone.

Short-term missions has outpaced long-term missions[2] in both personnel and budget. The North American church invests more money in short-term missions than in those who move overseas to live as missionaries. For a long time, the research done by missions scholars didn't reflect that shift and instead still focused primarily on long-term missions. However, the last five years have seen a surge in the number of studies that examine the effectiveness of short-term missions. Most of the research referenced in the chapters that follow comes from a variety of studies I've conducted on short-term missions.[3] I've also referenced some of the seminal studies conducted by other researchers.

With four to five million North Americans participating in short-term missions annually, it's unfair to generalize that my research represents every short-term missions experience. I'm not assuming that everything that follows applies to you or your team. At the same time, a number of us who have researched the short-term missions movement have been comparing our findings, and there's a consistency to what has emerged. So beware of too quickly writing off the critiques as not applying to you. Listen to the conflicting perspectives and pause to consider whether there's an element of truth in them for you or your team.

Part 2 is called "Conflicting Images." The reason will be obvious soon enough, but suffice it to say, many perceptions held by North Americans about short-term missions efforts are radically different from the perceptions of the majority world Christians who host these teams. There's some hard-hitting data in this section, but my intention is not to say that everyone who has done short-term missions has done it wrong. Instead, this section is meant to widen our perspective and improve the way we serve.

I've included something as part of the North American or majority world viewpoint only if it was voiced by enough people to make it a common theme. And alongside the words of caution voiced by majority world Christians were many positive things they said about short-term missions visitors. But since we aren't lacking for enthusiasm or confidence regarding the value of short-term missions, I've spent more time looking at the words of caution.

Our challenge in the North American church lies in putting our passports down long enough to take a closer look at what's going on in short-term missions. I'll tip my hand. I think there *is* a place for short-term missions, but I think many of our short-term missions efforts need to be rethought and reworked. Much of what follows could be confessional from my last twenty years of traveling the world. It's also a chronicle of how my own perspective has widened. I pray it will help you do the same. Open your eyes. Look at what you may have previously missed when looking at short-term missions.

3

Motivation

"Missions Should Be Fun!"

Through the eyes of North Americans . . .	Through the eyes of majority world Christians . . .
This trip isn't a "rough-roach-in-your-bed" kind of experience. We'll be housed in nice, clean hotel rooms, eat lots of salsa, and have plenty of time to shop![1]	Thousands of young men and women in China will go as missionaries who are not afraid to die for Jesus. They are not only willing to die for the gospel but also expecting it.[2]

I love to visit new places. Typically, when I travel overseas, I spend most of my day teaching or meeting inside sterile classrooms and offices. So when I get a few minutes to spare, I love to blaze the streets and take it all in. Where do the locals eat? Where do they hang out? What makes this place tick? What do people celebrate? What's the history of this city? I think this kind of desire to understand my surroundings has enhanced my ability to learn and serve in other places. At times, however, I'm challenged by a thought: Is my cross-cultural work driven most by my desire to follow Christ or by my sense of adventure and wanderlust?

What makes a short-term missions project different from a group who plans a tour through the same region? When is it mission, when is it vacation with a purpose, and when is it just vacation?

Sociologists have consistently found that the way we anticipate a situation strongly influences how we engage in it. More specifically, our expectations about a new role or a new environment will directly influence how we experience that new situation, both positively and negatively.

I've tried to incorporate this understanding into the counsel I give newly engaged couples. During premarital counseling, one of my priorities is to align the couple's expectations about marriage with reality. I remember all too well one of the comments Linda and I received while greeting guests at our wedding. A middle-aged woman walked up and said, with an incredibly sarcastic tone, "Well, those were nice, lofty vows. Now let's see if you can actually live up to them!" I waited for her to laugh, but she didn't! At the time I was annoyed. But as I look back on it now, I'm not sure she was trying to rain on our parade. Instead, I think she somehow found the need to warn us that marriage isn't purely romantic love songs lived out for forty years. I'm guessing she wanted us to adjust our expectations about marriage away from the romantic bliss of starry-eyed lovers to the realities of two unique individuals living together for the rest of our lives. Now, I don't recommend that kind of wedding etiquette any more than I encourage experienced parents to walk up to expectant mothers and tell them the horror stories of labor and sleepless nights awaiting them. But expectations do shape how we actually encounter new experiences.[3]

What are our expectations about short-term missions, and what motivates so many people to participate in such trips? That's what we'll explore in this chapter. Organizers and mission-trip recruiters play a significant role in shaping our expectations about short-term missions. When asked about the benefits of going or supporting those who go, people give myriad reasons. Most people promote short-term missions based on the way it will change the lives of both those who go and those who receive them. But other reasons that frequently surface in formal and informal discussions about short-term missions are the so-called biblical mandate for doing short-term missions and the adventure of the experience.

It's Biblical

The other day I had lunch with Debbie, a friend who is working hard to get her mega-church more involved in short-term missions projects. She said, "This Sunday I'm making another announcement. This time I'm going for the jugular. I'm going to say something like, 'This isn't just about whether or not you like Mexico or Romania or want to go there. It's a matter of obedience. God has commanded you to go. Short-term missions is about obeying the Great Commission.'"

"Wait a second, Debbie!" I replied. "Are you saying people who don't go on short-term missions trips are disobeying God?"

She backed off a little bit, but clearly she sees short-term missions as a matter of biblical obedience.

Debbie is in good company. Advocates of short-term missions often look to Scripture to demonstrate the biblical models of short-term missions. Roger Peterson, CEO and founder of STEM International, a short-term sending agency, says short-term missions is the *only* worldwide strategy that exists today to comply with the doctrine of the priesthood of believers—God using everyday people to fulfill his mission. Peterson and his fellow authors point to more than thirty "proof-text passages" (their words) for short-term missions. They range from the heavenly visitors who came to Abraham in the heat of the day (Gen. 18) to Nehemiah and the short-term construction mission (Neh. 2–10) to Jesus and the Samaritan woman at the well (John 4). Peterson is confident that short-term missions has a theological foundation that must not be ignored.[4]

Others have linked short-term missions to a strategy regularly employed by Jesus and Paul. For example, one missionary writes, "[The disciples] had watched [Jesus] sacrifice, serve, love, teach, and heal. They watched the Son of Man deal with popularity and opposition. It was time to send them out on their own short-term trip to copy the ministry that they had experienced."[5]

Does short-term missions violate Scripture? Not at face value, though many of the concerns I'm raising in this book need to be wrestled with in light of what God teaches us about being his physical presence in the world. However, might we need to use caution in too quickly using Scripture to legitimize short-term missions? What was the starting point for the short-term missions movement that has grown to such huge proportions today? Did it come from the conviction of men and women studying God's Word and discerning that this was a missing element in the church? Or was it a response to the increased accessibility we have to the world and a way to mobilize everyday people to experience missions firsthand? Clearly, we see people doing things itinerantly in many places throughout God's story, but ramping up short-term missions trips based on the belief that we're imitating Jesus's ministry can yield some dangerous practices.

It's an Adventure

On the other extreme lies the tension I personally feel as I think about my love for going new places. When is my drive to serve cross-culturally more a reflection of my desire for adventure than to truly engage in a noble endeavor? Is short-term missions simply a way of appeasing wanderlust?

The reports given by people before and after mission trips tend to emphasize the virtuous aspects: the number of souls saved, the lessons learned about prayer and materialism, and the impact made on the churches visited. However, sit down for coffee with a friend who has just returned from a trip or eavesdrop on the picture party of a returning group, and the adventure of life in a new place seems to be the emphasis. Such conversations are filled with stories about who got stopped going through customs, what it was like to eat the food, bartering the shopkeeper down to a ridiculous price, and experiencing the driving habits of the locals.

Let's be honest. Along with the seemingly more noble reasons for going on a short-term missions trip, the adventure of it all appeals to many of us. It's fun to fill up our passports with international stamps. As participants we try to be subtle about when and how often we ask the group leader about the plans for the "free time" on the trip, but we desperately want to know what new experiences we will have. We're told to make sure our reports back to the congregation focus on the "spiritual" things that happened—not just stories about getting sick and trying to speak the language. But there's an adventure that comes with traveling to a new place. Going to Mexico or Africa is much more exciting than going downtown.

Some organizations aren't subtle about using adventure and fun to motivate people to participate in short-term missions. For example, Teen Mania has been taking young people on mission trips for over twenty years. They report having sent sixty-five thousand short-term missionaries on projects called "Global Expeditions." They recently ran a full-page advertisement in a magazine for youth workers that featured this headline: "Missions Should Be Fun!" Below it was a picture of a group of North American youth pushing a cool-looking canoe down a tropical-like river with a few "natives" in tow.[6]

Teen Mania sends parents, youth leaders, and teenagers an eight-page, four-color brochure explaining all the details of "Global Expeditions." The headline of the brochure reads, "Missions Made Easy!" A picture below shows a North American youth group piled into a jeep that's roaming through high grasses. Turn the page and you see another large photo, this one of six North American teenagers standing below an exotic waterfall looking as if they're having the time of their lives.

This adventure-filled, fun-packed motif is often used by local church short-term-missions recruiters as well. Glenn Schwartz, executive director of World Missions Associates, shares the following excerpt from a church bulletin announcement about an upcoming trip to Mexico:

> [Our congregation] is sponsoring a women's-only mission trip to beautiful Guadalajara, Mexico! We'll spend the week of June 11–18 in Guadalajara (also known as the shopping capital of Mexico), where we will have the incredible opportunity to minister to, pray for, and teach women in a vibrant church community. And this trip isn't a "rough-roach-in-your-bed" kind of experience either. We'll be housed in nice, clean hotel rooms, eat lots of salsa, and have plenty of time to shop! Our hope is to take at least fifteen women (including teenager daughters) on this Mexican Ministry Outreach. . . . We trust that God will expand our hearts for Him as He expands our ministry to the women of Guadalajara. If you're remotely interested in this adventure—or if you're just in the mood for Mexico after all this winter weather—call for more details about this fantastic outreach opportunity.[7]

This fun-filled, adventurous mind-set is quite a contrast to that of the thousands of young, aspiring missionaries in China who are ready and expecting to die for the gospel during their mission sojourns. In their words, "The Muslim and Buddhist nations can torture us, imprison us, and starve us, but they can do no more than we have already experienced in China. . . . We are not only ready to die for the gospel, we are expecting it."[8]

A spirit of adventure and a desire to explore a new place aren't all bad. They can be part of how we open our eyes to the world in which we live. However, if the adventure of trekking through a new place is the primary drive behind our short-term missions experiences, we need to exercise caution. If adventure is most what you're after—go for it. Take a trip there! Explore the culture. Soak it in. Experience it fully. Just don't put a "mission trip" label on it and ask other people to fund it. Be "missional" when you go sightseeing in Prague or snorkel in Fiji. Always be looking for ways to call people to follow Jesus. Continually consider how to facilitate peace and justice. But let's beware of taking what ought to be normal activity for all of us everyday Christians and suddenly calling it a "mission project" and expecting other people to pay for it.

It Will Change Your Life

Obedience to a biblical mandate and pursuing a globe-trotting adventure are part of what motivates many Christians to participate in short-term missions. However, the main reason people participate in short-term missions is the life-changing experience it promises them.[9]

Think about your conversations with people after they return from a mission trip. Or consider your own descriptions of trips you've experienced. What's the most common response to the question, "How was your mission trip?" The response I hear more than any other is, "Life changing!" Spiritual growth is the very thing we're promised by many of the people who organize these trips: "This trip will change your life. You'll never view the world or your faith the same way again."

Most people are convinced short-term missions is one of the most effective ways to expose North American Christians to the needs of the world. An altered prayer life, a commitment to resist materialism, and a newfound orientation toward servanthood are all ways people describe the life change that occurs through short-term missions projects.[10]

Of the millions of North Americans participating in short-term missions projects every year, the majority are teenagers. Twenty-nine percent of US high school students have participated in one of these kinds of trips.[11] Almost any legitimate North American youth ministry is expected to have a mission trip as part of its annual program. In many cases, there's a six- or seven-year cycle of trips for students to engage in from middle school through high school. Mission trips have replaced the summer camp experience as the standard summer event for most North American youth groups.

Parents and leaders who struggle with why we're sending our kids overseas to engage in missions when we aren't doing it right in our own backyards are pacified with the assurance that one leads to the other. Mission trips are said to be the ideal vehicle to help students identify their own culture's consumerist and ethnocentric values, to respond to the needs of the world in ways that are faithful to their beliefs, and to challenge the status quo of how their culture shapes their lives.[12] Expose kids to the needs of the world, we're told, and they'll be much more engaged in serving their own communities when they come home.

Robert Bland, director of Teen Missions International, is reported as saying, "We tell our people who are leading our teams that we're building kids, not buildings. The purpose isn't just what we'll do for these people, but what these people will do for us. . . . There is not a single purpose in [short-term work] . . . but to us [building our kids] is the first purpose."[13]

Emphasizing how short-term missions trips can change the life of the "missionary" is a drastic change from what was historically emphasized in missions. Clearly, the goers have always experienced life change as a result of engaging in missions; however, investing billions of dollars in mission work that is *mostly* focused on the transformation of the missionary is a radical shift from the missions movement throughout church history. Most mission paradigms throughout the ages have called for long-term sacrifice for the sake of others.[14]

Many argue that while the focus may initially be on the short-term participant more than the receivers, a long-term vision is required. As short-term participants become engaged in mission, get a view for the world, and personally experience life change, the receivers benefit in the long run. Short-term participants are prime candidates for becoming career missionaries. So while the first purpose of short-term missions for people such as Bland may be changing North American kids, I expect he, as others, would say that in the long term it will result in changing the lives of people elsewhere.

But a growing number of researchers question the long-term impact of short-term trips on participants. Some studies demonstrate that while participants come home with lofty aspirations of buying less, praying more, and sharing Christ more, within six to eight weeks most resort back to the same assumptions and behaviors they had prior to the trip.[15] And the number of North American Christians pursuing long-term careers as missionaries is getting smaller while the number of people participating in short-term missions is getting bigger. Something doesn't add up.

Others are even more critical about the impact of short-term missions on many who go. David Maclure contends that not only do these trips fail to bring about lasting life change for the participants, but, worse yet, they also actually perpetuate the very things they're intended to counter. Participants come home assuming that poor people are doing just fine and are happy that way and that developing countries are backward, given their chaotic road systems and archaic ways of doing construction. "Instead of advancing the cause of mission, the exercise simply reinforces worn stereotypes and old power relations."[16]

So which is it? Do short-term missions trips change our lives when we go or not? Before you jump to your own experiences to defend your answer, let's hold off on trying to answer the question right now. Instead, let's pay attention to these dissenting perspectives to open our eyes.

It Will Change Their Lives

The other leading motivation for short-term missions is the chance to make an impact on the lives and communities of people around the world. Participants are excited about the chance to leave the mundane world of life at home to travel to a different place to share the gospel, build a building, or teach a workshop. The kinds of activities in which short-term missions groups engage are diverse. Individuals and teams do everything from conducting medical clinics and evangelistic meetings to performing drama and music to building homes and painting churches.

When short-term participants seek financial and prayer support, they most strongly emphasize the benefit to the recipients. A few of the support letters I've received recently included statements such as the following:

- "Many of the people devastated by the tsunami are not getting the help they need. We have a chance to rebuild the homes of the homeless in Japan."
- "Most of the Brazilian churches don't have [church] buildings like we do. Our team is excited to build this [Brazilian] congregation a new building where they can meet."
- "We'll be running a vacation Bible school for the children."
- "Ireland is a place without God. Pray for us as we bring the gospel there."
- "This will be the first church ever built in this city."

These are the kinds of sentiments that permeate the pleas of short-term participants seeking support. Such expectations are at the core of students leaving the comforts of suburban North America to mix cement for a week in Mexico. These assumptions are part of why giving to short-term missions now exceeds giving to long-term missions.

The assumption that a short-term trip can make a significant impact on those on the receiving end is held not only by high school students and laypeople. More and more North American pastors travel overseas regularly to conduct training workshops. The following comments are typical of what I've heard from North American leaders who participate in these kinds of experiences:

- "I'm excited to equip these leaders [in Columbia] so they can be more effective in their youth ministries. I know how these principles have benefited us, so think about the benefit to them!"

- "I'm so excited . . . to take what God's done in our ministry here and multiply it to other places."
- "I would imagine these youth workers have lots of great ideas, but do they have a philosophy of ministry? I would guess they don't. I want them to walk away with a good structure for ministry."
- "We have a chance to bring Spirit-filled worship to Indonesia. The tiny Christian church there needs the power of prayer released."
- "This is the first time this kind of church-planting training has ever been offered in south India."

These participants wanted to see their own lives changed, but most of all they wanted to change the lives of others. Their mentality is, "We don't do short-term missions for the fun and excitement, or because everyone else is doing it, or because we're told we have to go. *We go to serve and share.*"[17]

While the life-changing impact of these trips on the locals is used as a way to motivate people to support the trips, little research has explored whether short-term trips really help the cause of the global church as much as we think. Most of the reports about the positive impact on local communities come from North American participants and sponsoring organizations, not from those who received the participants.

Those who have researched the impact of short-term missions on the receivers aren't convinced that these trips are changing the recipients. One missionary says, "Everyone knows that short-term missions benefit the people who come, not the people here."[18] In fact, many missionaries are concerned that the very nature of a short-term trip creates a temporary approach to things that require more long-term solutions.

Kurt VerBeek, a sociologist living in Honduras, is one of the few researchers studying the impact of short-term missions on local communities. VerBeek studied a North American relief organization's role in helping Hondurans rebuild their homes after Hurricane Mitch in 1998. The organization raised over 2 million dollars for reconstruction of 1.5 million homes lost and channeled it through Honduran partners. In turn, these partners hired Honduran builders to work with people to rebuild their homes. In addition, the organization mobilized thirty-one short-term teams from the United States and Canada to assist in rebuilding homes. VerBeek was interested in whether there was a greater impact made on the Honduran communities that received short-term groups compared to those who received homes built by Honduran builders with North American money.

Through the data collected, VerBeek found no lasting difference, positive or negative, on the Honduran families and communities whose homes were built by North Americans compared to those who never saw a short-term missions team. In fact, in a moment of candidness, the Hondurans confided that if given the choice, they'd rather see the money raised by each team who traveled to Honduras channeled toward building twenty more homes and employing Hondurans.[19]

At the very least, we need to resist the temptation to overstate our level of impact. Our desire to inspire our friends and family members often leads us to give the impression that what we did was the first, best, biggest, and most effective such effort ever accomplished in this place.

The findings and critiques of researchers and majority world church leaders should make us more cautious in our language. Is God really not in Ireland? Are we really introducing worship to the Indonesian church, one of the fastest-growing churches in the world despite the immense amount of persecution there? Are we teaching south Indians to plant churches, or given the rate of growth in their church-planting movements, should they be teaching us a few things about church planting?

Accuracy or inaccuracy of such statements is not my primary concern. What do these assumptions do to influence how we engage in short-term endeavors? How do our expectations shape the way we come across to the local believers who receive and host us? When we fail to step back and serve with eyes wide open, we cause many local pastors to feel as this African leader did after hosting an American pastor who came to train African church leaders for a few days. "He never once asked to see anything that I had done—that just made me feel like nothing we have is worth anything." If our eyes are open to the realities of the majority world church considered earlier, it will change the expectations that shape our engagement.

Concluding Thoughts

We need to open our eyes to see how our motivation for short-term missions influences how we engage in our ministry and service. Be encouraged. Honesty about what does and doesn't occur through short-term missions allows us to see our trips as an integral part of our lifelong journey of following Jesus rather than just a two-week project. As we take our eyes off ourselves and begin to look outward, we see our short-term experiences as a way to encounter God's work in local churches around the world.

Conflicting perspectives on why we should participate in short-term missions is the most important place to begin to serve with eyes wide open. We'll revisit the motivational aspects of service in part 3 as we explore improving our CQ for serving cross-culturally.

4

Urgency

"Just Do It!"

Through the eyes of North Americans . . .	Through the eyes of majority world Christians . . .
We've got to do something. The window of opportunity is *now*! The time for change is ripe. We must seize this opportunity.	You too quickly get into the action without thinking through the implications for our churches long after you go home.

Time—it's a precious thing. Rarely is a day of my life not carefully scheduled. Even my vacation days are twenty-four-hour time blocks to be conquered. After all, planning our family vacation is a way to be sure our family maximizes our "play time" together. I pride myself on getting a lot done in a day's work. I'm obsessed with efficiency. I stand in line and come up with ways things could be done better and quicker. Ah yes, when it comes to time, I'm terminally American, though admittedly, not every American is as obsessed with efficiency as I am.

Seizing the moment and making a difference are compelling forces in our cross-cultural experiences. Clearly, this can be a good thing. There are urgent needs that need strategic intervention. But if we aren't careful, our desire to jump in and do something efficient can reflect a human-centered approach to missions rather than a God-centered one.

This chapter explores our North American tendency to take action and take charge of a situation before fully understanding the context. North Americans as a whole and particularly North American Christians are not known for reflection or for pausing to think through the long-term consequences of our actions. Let's explore this and compare it with how Jesus approaches the issue of urgency and time.

The North American Way

Think of the number of clichés and proverbs that are part of our everyday vocabulary. We put huge value on time. We believe it's a scarce, valuable resource. We say:

> "Time is money."
> "We need to do this sooner rather than later."
> "There's no time like the present."
> "Make every minute count."
> "It's now or never."
> "Haste makes waste."
> "The early bird catches the worm."

Our North American obsession with time and urgency makes us want to schedule and control everything. Long gone are the days when kids made the best of playing with the neighbors next door. We schedule play dates and organize "community" with fellow church members in small groups. Our lives are so packed that we need vacations to get away from home, but even our vacations are often full of one planned event after another. An urgency drives the North American way, part of which is a gift we can offer the global church. Our history as a land of pioneering immigrants who rebelled against the Old World has allowed us to be a force for good in the world. We don't merely sit back and talk about how things could be different; we make them different. We take charge of situations and seize the moment.

Our obsession with making the most of every opportunity and the entrepreneurial spirit of our North American heritage are not without positive impact, but they are also loaded with problems. Our pillaging of Native American land and culture to make a place for ourselves was deplorable. Our frequent unwillingness to collaborate in a global process that takes more time and effort often results in death—literally! Our drive to make everything happen now rather than seeing what unfolds can lead us to be judgmental of people in more laid-back cultures.

Richard Dooling's novel *White Man's Grave* is a riveting story about Michael Killigan, a Peace Corps volunteer who goes missing in West Africa. Michael's best friend, Boone, leaves Indiana to go to Sierra Leone to look for Michael. With good reason, Boone has a sense of urgency about finding out what's happened to his friend. His urgency goes beyond his immediate mission, however. He applies it to everything he encounters in Sierra Leone. For example, one day Boone observes a baby who isn't breathing normally, and he says, "I can't stand it. I have to do something." In response to Boone's urgency, his African host says:

> "That's when white people are most dangerous. When they try to make things 'better' for Africans. When white people are trying to enslave Africans or rob them, the Africans usually know what to do. They've dealt with slave traders, invaders, and plunderers for centuries. They usually quench the world's thirst for slaves by capturing some of their enemies and selling them to slave traders. But when white people come in with a lot of money or 'know-how' and try to make things 'better,' that's when things go to hell. Why can't white people just visit? Why must they always meddle? It's as if you were invited to dinner at someone's house and during your brief visit you insisted on rearranging all the furniture in the house to suit your tastes."[1]

Urgency, taking charge, and making the most of every opportunity—they're part of what it means to be a North American.

The Evangelical Way

The activist, urgent, take-charge ethos of North American culture is mirrored in the subculture of North American evangelicalism. Pragmatism—doing whatever works in the most efficient way—rules the day in most North American churches. Our inspiration and zeal overpower our ability to step back and engage in serious reflection. We struggle with a messiah complex that Jesus himself never had, and he *was* the Messiah!

The question that has dominated much of North American evangelicalism over the last several decades is, "What works?" Success is measured and defended based on effectiveness and efficiency. If preaching doesn't draw a crowd, then figure out what will. If the symbol of the cross or reciting creeds hinders someone from coming to church, get rid of them. Business practices based on urgency and efficiency drive the agendas of many churches.[2]

A great deal of our evangelical urgency stems from this mind-set: "Hurry up and get to work for Jesus! The clock is ticking." Urgency is central to our approaches to missions. For example, the AD 2000 movement was a significant force in missions at the end of the twentieth century. AD 2000 called the global church to embrace the vision to see a church for every people and the gospel for every person by the year 2000. There was an appropriate desire to work harder to focus our resources and attention on the people who had yet to hear about Jesus. At times, however, this much-needed focus on the unreached peoples of the world translated into some very human-centered plans for living out God's mission.

The short-term missions movement itself was built on a sense of urgency. George Verwer, founder of Operation Mobilization, was frustrated by the time it took to mobilize adults from the West for the mission field. He saw the vastness of the need to evangelize and wanted to get at the task now! He was impatient to get on with the work by every means at his disposal.

As Verwer looked around, it seemed the people with the most availability were college students on summer vacation. So he came up with a plan to forgo using traditional missionaries and instead mobilize college students to get at the job. In his mind, this was a lot more effective than looking for someone who would have to be uprooted from a job and a house and spend time learning a language. The short-term missions movement has grown astronomically in the fifty years since then.

The very title of one book—*Maximum Impact, Short-Term Mission*—assumes an urgency to what we're doing. The authors write, "For every additional hour required of preparation, for every additional characteristic demanded of recruits, there will be thousands—perhaps millions?—who remain sidelined as too average, too real, too foolish to that particular expression of 'Missio Dei.' In our feeble attempts to birth a missionary without spot or blemish, the world continues to go to hell without Jesus."[3]

The North American pastors I studied demonstrated a strong sense of urgency in their international training efforts. One pastor said, "If all the other countries get on board with what we're training . . . we could see the return of Christ much sooner, possibly even this generation." He believed his training efforts could expedite the return of Christ. Though most of the pastors studied didn't defend urgency quite that way, nearly all of them did embrace a desire to see measurable results, something that allowed for a laser focus on seeing maximum impact in a short amount of time.

In contrast, here are the kinds of comments I heard as I collected data from our brothers and sisters in majority world churches when they spoke about short-term missions:

- "You too quickly get into the action without thinking through the implications for our churches long after you go home."
- "You come here for two weeks. We're here forever. We're not as panicked about finishing all the projects as soon as you are."
- "You assume we aren't focused because we haven't written up our mission, vision, and values like you have. But we are very clear about what God is doing in our midst."
- "Your strategies and plans are helpful. But where's the Holy Spirit?"

It's hard to respond to the world's needs without a certain degree of urgency. But when does our urgency cause more harm than good?

Jesus's Way

When looking at Jesus's approach to life, we find an interesting tension between his ruthless focus on an urgent mission and his ability to take time for "interruptions." Clearly, there was a sense of urgency in how he went about mission, but he didn't seem to talk about it with an overly designed strategy or with a clock ticking in the background. This is evident as far back as his childhood.

By age twelve Jesus was hanging out in the Jerusalem temple talking with the Jewish leaders. The temple was by far the largest religious structure in the world, known widely for its wealth and magnitude. Jerusalem was more like a temple with a city around it than a city with a temple in it. The temple was the center of religious, social, and political activity—the epicenter of the entire nation.

So it was a pretty big deal for a twelve-year-old Jewish boy to wax eloquently with the esteemed leaders of Jerusalem. If Jesus operated in the "North American way," perhaps his reasoning about his experience in the temple would have gone something like this: "This is a God thing. The window of opportunity is now! It's not every day a young Jewish boy gets an audience with the movers and shakers of Israel. So I need to forgo this carpentry stuff with my dad and leverage this opportunity. There's no time like the present. Carpe diem!"

Yet as far as we know, Jesus spent the next eighteen years secluded with his simple family in lowly Nazareth. Even as the Son of God, Jesus didn't forgo the necessity of preparation, which mainly took place out of the public eye. And though Jesus didn't demand perfection out of those he called to join him in mission, he also didn't seem to be in a hurry to get them to the task at hand.

Jesus also didn't seem to be very good at closing the deal with people. He often walked away from people after having left them with a rather nebulous statement. That doesn't seem like maximum-impact short-term missions to me. Yet somehow Jesus seemed to believe that the Father was capable of continuing redemptive work in the lives of people long after he "walked away" from them.

Once Jesus embarks on his public ministry, Luke keeps reminding us that Jesus *did* have a destination. Again and again Luke tells us that Jesus was "making his way to Jerusalem." Here are just a few examples:

Jesus resolutely set out for Jerusalem.

Luke 9:51

Jesus went through the towns . . . as he made his way to Jerusalem.

Luke 13:22

Now on his way to Jerusalem . . .

Luke 17:11

Jesus took the Twelve aside and told them, "We are going up to Jerusalem."

Luke 18:31

Jesus . . . went on ahead, going up to Jerusalem.

Luke 19:28

Jesus is pretty clear about his destination. He has to get to Jerusalem. The destination of a lifetime awaits him there. So there's clarity about his mission and its urgency. Everything runs through the filter of getting to Jerusalem. But his sense of urgency doesn't prevent him from being compassionate, generous, and spontaneous. Along the way he heals countless people, he teaches his disciples and the crowds who gather to see him, and he doesn't seem hurried or panicked.[4]

What a different picture from how I live. What a contrast to the urgency that seems to drive some of our assumptions about what we must do when we engage in missions cross-culturally.

Concluding Thoughts

The very nature of short-term projects in and of themselves brings a sense of urgency. When we're engaged with a group of people or in a region for only a short amount of time, we have an even greater sense of needing to make the time count. In listening to short-term participants throughout the years, I've often heard, "We've got to do something. The window of opportunity is *now*! The time for change is ripe. We must seize this opportunity."

There is certainly some value to the urgency that characterizes the North American church. Frankly, I think our ability to offer vision, planning, and direction to the dreams of others is one of the most valuable contributions we can offer the global church, but we must do so carefully. It must happen in ways that are shaped by the local church that was there long before we arrived and will be there long after we leave. Most of all, we must not live as if God's mission is somehow contingent upon our plans and strategies. Jesus remains on the throne and continues his redemptive work with or without our frantic sense of urgency.

5

Common Ground

"They Don't Fly Planes in India When It Rains"

Through the eyes of North Americans . . .	Through the eyes of majority world Christians . . .
If there were any surprises for me, it came in how similar everything is to everything back home.	I might look like the kids in your neighborhood on the outside. But what's on the inside is totally different.

I had just finished speaking at a conference in St. Louis, and Mike, a twenty-two-year-old Christian college student, was elected to drive me to the airport. It was pouring rain.

"It's a good thing you aren't in India right now," Mike said.

"Why?" I asked.

"Because they don't fly planes in India when it rains," he replied.

"Really?!" I responded. "What makes you say that?"

"Well, I just spent two weeks there. We had a couple domestic flights, and whenever it was raining, they canceled our flights. I guess they don't have the technology we do for flying in this kind of stuff."

I couldn't decide whether to smile and nod or tell him about the countless times I've taken off from Indian airports in the midst of torrential downpours.

We have a strong tendency to overgeneralize our unique cross-cultural experiences because of a desire to find common ground and make the foreign seem familiar. There are a couple ways this gets played out in short-term missions. One tendency is to look for the similarities between the new culture and something we've experienced before—usually our home culture or another foreign culture we've encountered. The other way we try to establish common ground is by taking isolated incidents or people and applying what we see in them to everything or everyone in a culture. This is one of the most common pitfalls we make when we encounter a new cultural context.[1]

How are we the same? How are we different? What's an isolated incident or behavior, and what's typical of a culture as a whole? These are some of the most important things to consider as we widen our perspective. We're going to get at this topic in two ways: (1) our tendency to look for similarities and (2) our tendency to apply an isolated event or trait to an entire culture.

People Are People

Eastern or Western, rich or poor, black or white, people are people. Sure, there are differences, but at the end of the day, we as human beings are more alike than different. This prevailing assumption drives the tendency to seek common ground.

More than three-quarters of the short-term participants I surveyed commented on the similarities they observed in the new culture with what they experienced at home or in another place. Often this response came in reply to the question, "What surprised you most about your trip?" Here are a few of the responses:

- "Maybe the real point is that they just aren't as different from us as I thought they would be. Or maybe it's that in spite of a few superficial differences, like clothes and food, they are more like us than I thought."
- "I understand more of what is going on than I expected to (not the language of course, but the things people do). I watched people in the restaurant the other night, and there was nothing they did I wouldn't do back home."

- "We're all fallen people, and the issues are much the same because we have the same root to deal with [sin]. I prepared myself for all the differences, but I don't think I needed to. We're a lot more alike than different."

- "They struggle with the same things in their churches as we do—elder boards, parents, how to get people to buy into the vision, sacred cows, that kind of stuff. It sounds a whole lot like our church!"

- "The students I taught met most of my expectations. . . . If there were any surprises for me, it came in how similar they and the issues they're dealing with are to the students I teach back home."

Why are we so inclined to find similarities between us and those we meet in new places? Are our perceptions about our sameness accurate? At face value, there's value in our desire to find "sameness" in our fellow citizens of the globe. We are all created in the image of God. We all long to love and be loved. We were all created for a mission and to have purpose. We're all born and we'll all die. Our common bond as humans is evident during crises such as an earthquake or a tsunami. Suddenly, the Islamic-Buddhist-Christian, male-female, East-West barriers are diminished. We watch with horror as our fellow human beings are destroyed by a natural disaster. When we begin to see what we have in common with each other as humans rather than being obsessed with the differences, we begin to strip away the "us versus them" mentality.

In fact, looking for common ground with our fellow citizens of the globe is a normal and healthy way of coping with the inevitable dissonance that occurs when we encounter a new culture. Traveling to a new place brings on an irresistible impulse to smooth over the strangeness. We look for similarities because it's reassuring for us to spot something familiar when we go somewhere for the first time. Before we know it, however, we become so focused on the similarities that we fail to marvel at the differences. Only when we've been in a new culture long enough to be repeatedly shocked at the error of our assumptions do we begin to see the things we missed before.[2]

A great deal of research has been done on culture shock and examining the cycles that typically occur for someone encountering a new culture for the first time. Finding common ground is the coping mechanism most often used in the first several weeks in a new place. After a couple months of being immersed in a new culture, one begins to see all the differences rather than the similarities. However, most short-term participants aren't in a new culture long enough to experience this shift. We're back to life as normal long before we experience the depths of the differences that become apparent after more extended cross-cultural immersions.

The brevity of our cross-cultural experiences ought to alert us to the wrong conclusions we make as a result of the common-ground issue. Many of the behaviors, nonverbal cues, and issues we observe may in fact be familiar. The question lies in whether they mean the same thing in a different culture. When we're in a cross-cultural context for only a brief period of time, we interpret everything we see through our own cultural framework rather than learning, over time, to identify with another cultural framework. As a result, a short-term trip has the potential of further reinforcing inaccurate assumptions and interpretations rather than helping alter our inaccurate assumptions. Even multiple short trips to the same place don't necessarily alter them. Continued brief encounters in the same place often result in continued observation of the same similarities rather than exposing the vastly different cultural paradigms at work.

An Indiana youth group who traveled to Ecuador for a couple weeks described the consistent joy and contentment evident among their Ecuadorian hosts. In struggling to overcome the language barrier, students found themselves doing a lot of waving and smiling to their Latin hosts; the Ecuadorians reciprocated with equally warm smiles and waves. As a result, the students talked a great deal about the unusual measure of joy and contentment among the Ecuadorian people as a whole. They talked about the amazing love of Ecuadorians for Americans.

Terry Linhart, a researcher and professor of youth ministry, joined this group on their trip to Ecuador as a way to better understand the short-term mission phenomenon. Linhart compares the high school students' interaction with the Ecuadorians to an interactive museum. The students gawked at the "living artifacts" from Ecuador without really encountering them. The North Americans worshiped alongside the Ecuadorians, performed for them, and poured out affection on their children. However, with limited ability to cross the chasm of language, the students were unable to make accurate perceptions about the Latinos. Linhart writes, "Without spending significant time with the person, visiting his or her home, or even possessing rudimentary knowledge about the person's history, students made quick assessments of their hosts' lives and values."[3] Their reasoning went something like this: "When we smile and show friendliness, that means we're happy. It's a sign of joy. Therefore, these people's wide smiles and aggressive waves clearly prove the contentment and joy of all Ecuadorians."

But we must be cautious about too quickly interpreting the meaning behind nonverbal behaviors. Smiles and laughter in another culture may in fact be signs of joy, but they may just as likely be responses to an awkward situation in which words cannot be used due to a language barrier. Likewise, a nonverbal response of silence or a lack of nodding one's head in agreement doesn't necessarily mean under-standing *isn't* taking place.

I often observe this when African-American preachers speak to predominantly Anglo audiences. It's widely known that many African-American congregations are very expressive as they listen to their preachers. I feel for the African-American preachers who move from that setting to a stuffy white one. At times, however, I've been among the white audiences who have received a tongue-lashing from preach-ers who assume we're apathetic and disinterested because we don't respond with shouts and nods. Many of these preachers interpret the nonverbal cues they receive based on what they mean in their own cultural context. The reasoning goes something like this: "When my people are bored and disengaged, they don't say anything. Therefore, this white crowd's silence means they're bored and disengaged."

I've often done the same thing when teaching cross-culturally. When I teach, I draw a lot of my energy from how the students respond ver-bally and nonverbally. Furthermore, this is one of the primary ways I assess whether learning is occurring. I've spent a great deal of time teaching in Asian contexts where the level of immediate responsive-ness is far less apparent than what I experience in North American teaching contexts. Even though I know that, and even though I'm writing about it right now, next week when I'm teaching in Asia, this issue will continue to be an ongoing challenge for me.

Misreading cross-cultural behavior is one of the most consistent findings of my research. The most frequent statement made by the North American pastors I studied was, "These people are so hungry for our training!" Every pastor/trainer said something like the following:

- "They were really hungry [for the training]."
- "The training [was] outstanding. . . . I think they were hungry, very hungry. I would even say more hungry overseas than they are here . . . because they're looking for more effective ways and tools."
- "They would sit and listen. They wouldn't get up and go to the bathroom every five minutes or say, "I need a break" every couple hours. They were enduring heat . . . humidity . . . the small environment. . . . And they didn't get up and leave. I mean they were spellbound . . . in listening to the message, the methodology . . . the format . . . the how to's, and the philosophy."
- "It was fresh and new [like] they had never heard it before. They really soaked it in."
- "They were so thirsty. They just hung on every word."

I asked the trainers how they came to these conclusions. Responses ranged from "I just sensed it from the questions they asked and from the way they listened so intently" to "I asked them if they were tracking and they said yes." Others drew upon nonverbal feedback, concluding that nodding heads and note taking implied learning was occurring.

In contrast, the most brutally honest student who sat in this training said, "You conclude you're communicating effectively because we're paying attention when we're actually just intrigued by watching your foreign behavior." This African leader wasn't the only one who made a statement challenging the assumptions of the American trainers. Some of the other statements made by the local ministry leaders who sat in the training included:

- "It was a nice day, but I don't think what they taught would ever work here. But if it makes them feel like they can help us in ways beyond supporting our ministry financially, we're willing to listen to their ideas."

- "I'm glad the trainers felt respected. They should. What they need to realize, however, is that we would never think about talking or getting up to leave in the middle of their lecture. It would be repulsive to do that to a teacher in our culture."
- "I wish we could have shared more about the real challenges we're facing in our ministry. How do I lead a church when most of our godly men have lost their lives in battle? How do I help a parent care for their AIDS baby? Those are my pressing issues, not growing my church bigger or starting a second service. I didn't get that whole discussion."

While hesitant to be overly critical, more than half of the local pastors studied expressed frustration that North American pastors talked about successful churches in the United States with little awareness of many churches that are far bigger in other parts of the world. And as a result of striving to find common ground, many North American pastors felt that the needs among the local pastors were the same as those back home. Almost every North American pastor commented on the similarity in the issues in churches cross-culturally. Whether discussing youth ministry, elder boards, getting people to buy into a vision, putting people under church discipline, or dealing with ex-pectations people have for the pastor, most of the North Americans concluded, "Church is church, wherever you go."

Perhaps this explains why one Brazilian pastor described his frustration with what occurred when he attended the training done by a North American as follows:

During our class, I was describing some of the challenges our church is facing in our Bible study groups. I shared how our adolescents rarely feel free to speak up because of some dominant older members. The trainer immediately started to tell me why this proves our need for a specific program for the young people. I told him we're resisting that trend because we want to keep the generations together. He laughed and said, "That's where the American church was forty years ago, but you're going to have to develop a strong youth ministry or you'll lose those kids."

Conflicting perspectives between North American trainers and majority world church pastors were more than occasional. During my extended study and review, these two very different perspectives became a consistent theme. North American pastors operate on the assumption that "things here are pretty much the same as at home, so these pastors are really hungry for guidance on how to lead." In contrast, the local pastors who received them said, "You act as if the North American church is the true trendsetter for how we should all do church."

I would be misrepresenting majority world Christians to suggest that nothing of value comes from this kind of training or that it's always a waste of time. Several pastors described specific experiences with foreign teachers that really moved them forward in their lives and ministries. So while you may be ready to ban everyone from short-term training efforts overseas, I'm not ready to go there just yet. The point is not that nothing good ever comes from the trips or the training. Instead, how might our widened perspective improve the way we engage and serve?

One short-term participant said, "I wish I had spent less time studying the cultural differences because I was really more struck by the similarities than the differences." On the other hand, a short-term participant who exercised cultural intelligence made perhaps the most accurate and appropriate statement in relation to this topic when he said, "They are just like us but not like us at all."

"Everyone" Here Is . . .

When we can't find similarities between ourselves and the people we encounter in a new place, we seek common ground by making generalizations about all events and people in a new place. This is what my airport driver did when he assumed that rainy skies in India equals grounded planes.

According to Linhart's analysis of the Indiana youth group's experience in Ecuador, all the students on the trip, except one, seemed unaware of the myriad of Ecuadorians who passed each day. These locals seemed to contradict the way the students were interpreting the smiles and waves they received from their hosts. Linhart says the Ecuadorians in general appeared "uninterested in the group, or portrayed facial expressions that were quite different from those who served as the hosts of the group."[4] Even if the high school students accurately perceived the contentment and joy of their hosts, they moved into unfounded territory when they declared that all Ecuadorians are like this.

Linhart is careful to qualify his analysis by saying that the students' intentions were honorable and compassionate. Part of the challenge came in the sheer brevity of the experience, which fostered a near necessity to stereotype—to reduce people to a few simple, essential characteristics. Fill in the blanks: "Italians are all _____." "Indian people are always so _____." "Of course he'll be late, he's _____." On second thought, don't fill in the blanks! Probably several of us would finish those sentences the same way. Stereotypes are ingrained in our perceptions about others. They are based on taking a few simple, vivid, memorable characteristics of people we've experienced or heard about in a particular place and making those common to everyone there. We tend to reduce everything about people in a culture to the few simple stereotypes we have of them.[5]

Nonjudgmental stereotyping can assist us in cross-cultural engagement. Understanding familiar traits and values of a particular culture helps us interact more effectively there. For example, if we understand the way most Latins think about time as compared to how we do, or if we think about the communal orientation of most Africans compared to our individualistic drive, or if we consider the respect given to elders in an Asian context, it will help move us toward cultural intelligence. The challenge lies in whether our stereotypes are accurate generalizations in the first place and whether they apply to a particular individual we encounter.

At best, the key lies in holding nonjudgmental stereotypes loosely and not applying them too quickly to everyone. We must beware of having an experience with one or two individuals from a particular place and suddenly thinking we've experienced a characteristic that can be applied to all or even most people from that place. And we ought to resist creating stereotypes on our own but instead look for what extended research about a particular culture suggests. Some things about me are terminally North American, but other aspects of my personality are unique to me as an individual. The same is true of you. The same is true of the people we encounter when we travel to a new place.

Concluding Thoughts

One day I was at a bus stop in Kuala Lumpur, Malaysia. Standing
next to me was an eighteen-year-old Malay guy dressed in an Aber-
crombie & Fitch sweatshirt, Diesel jeans, and a baseball cap. With
his backpack over his shoulder and sipping his Starbucks mocha, he
pulled the ear buds from his ears and we began talking. Soon into the
conversation, he asked me what the kids his age are like in my North
American neighborhood back home. I started by saying, "Well, you
could easily be mistaken for one of them. A lot of them look just
like you." He laughed, and we continued talking for another fifteen
minutes after boarding the same bus. As my new friend got up to exit
the bus, he turned to me and said, "Just remember, sir, I might look
like the kids in your neighborhood on the outside. But what's on the
inside is totally different." If I wasn't convinced before he made the
statement, I was then! Our conversation itself was different from what
I typically have with teenagers in my neighborhood.

Looking for common ground isn't a bad thing. I actually find it
quite inspiring to think about the connection we have with people
everywhere. We can find common ground not only with Christians
everywhere but also with all our fellow image bearers in the world. We
share similar fears, loves, and needs. There's something right about
seeing our similarities. But we're wise to discover and embrace the
differences between us as well! It's part of serving with eyes wide open.

6

The Bible

"Just Stick to the Bible and You Can't Go Wrong!"

Through the eyes of North Americans . . .	Through the eyes of majority world Christians . . .
We came here to teach about the life of Christ and how he did ministry. So cultural differences really don't matter.	I have never met anyone more insensitive to a local culture, but he said he is transcultural and that he is not American but *biblical* in his values.

I usually get a great deal of agreement, affirming nods, and empathetic gasps for the kinds of things I've shared in the last few chapters—challenging our reasons for engaging in short-term missions, tempering our urgency, and questioning what we assume to be "common." However, this next issue—the different perspectives surrounding the Bible—tends to be the one with which many Christians struggle most. Many thoughtful missionaries and leaders have said to me, "I agree wholeheartedly with the things you've been talking about thus far. Our cultural assumptions are dangerous and lead to all kinds of problems. But how can you say that biblical principles aren't cross-cultural? They are!" The mantra that drives most mission work is this: "Methods are many; principles are few. Methods always change, but principles never do."

I realize that challenging the mantra that "biblical principles never change" can seem like dangerous territory, but we have to go there if we're serious about widening our perspective for doing short-term missions. The deep-rooted influence of culture goes far beyond the foods we eat, the ways we celebrate holidays, and whether we're chronically "late." Culture shapes the way we think; it alters how and what we learn. Two individuals can receive the same information, and their respective cultures can lead them to arrive at two entirely different conclusions.

Culture's influence on scriptural interpretation was the issue a group of Western missionaries in Africa were interested in exploring with some of the African pastors. The group brought in an outside facilitator. The first thing the missionaries and pastors were asked to do was write down what they considered to be the central message of the story of Joseph in Genesis. The missionaries agreed that the story of Joseph was a picture of a man who was loyal to God even to the point of resisting the most intense measure of sexual temptation. The Africans, however, concluded that Joseph was a picture of a man who in spite of his brothers' mistreatment remained intensely loyal to his family.[1] What's the "right" interpretation of this ancient story?

Culture is one of many dynamics that influence how we interpret Scripture. Our personality, our family background, our social class, our church experience, and much more shape how we understand truth and interpret the Bible.

Let's look specifically at the role of culture in how we read the Bible. We're going to explore this in three ways: seeing the Bible differently, looking at the danger of "biblical" models, and moving toward a multicultural view of Scripture. It all starts with the question, "What is the Bible?"

Seeing the Bible Differently

I grew up being taught that the Bible is the answer book. We focused on fundamentals such as inerrancy, authority of Scripture, infallibility, objectivity, and absolute and literal interpretation. The Bible was described as a rule book with clear-cut categories. There was very little room for gray, and we positioned ourselves against so-called Christian groups that arrived at interpretations different from ours—whether concerning the end times or women in leadership.

On the other end of the spectrum were the so-called liberals who saw the Bible as the story of Israel's experience that had some symbolic and allegorical application for today. The miracles weren't historically accurate but rather images and metaphors that could teach us something about life with God.

As I began traveling the world and interacting with Christians in different places, neither my fundamentalist perspective nor the so-called liberal stance seemed to represent the view of the Bible I encountered among many Christians overseas. Reducing the Bible to a rule book or a manual for the Christian life didn't seem like a very high view of Scripture. On the other hand, why would I give my life to obey words that were merely symbolic in nature, much less challenge others to do so?

I began to see that the Bible itself was not the *end* but rather a *means* to the end—Jesus! I'm not saying the Bible is unimportant. In fact, I'm calling for a heightened view of Scripture that sees it for all it is.[2]

In our obsession with making the Bible the end-all rather than a means to the end, we've imported far too much Western culture into understanding the purpose of the Scriptures. In a quest for certainty, we've often treated the Bible as God's scientific encyclopedia and how-to guide for Christian living, a view similar to that of the scribes and Pharisees in Jesus's day.

The Bible is true and reliable. It's also far *more* than a rule book! It's the story of God! It's God's telling of history. It's messy. It includes God drowning most of humanity and the killing of Egyptian babies. It calls David—a powerful king who murdered a man and committed adultery—a "man after God's own heart." I don't get all that. But I refuse to rob God's story of the mystery by neatly explaining it all away. We have to embrace the Bible for all it is and be on a lifelong quest to deepen our understanding of it as a way to know and follow Christ.

Part of seeing the Bible differently means moving away from being predominantly interested in what the Bible means for *us* and moving toward a growing interest in what the Bible meant in its *original* context. Only through this kind of rigorous historical work can we move toward a fuller comprehension of what the authors themselves were trying to say. The challenge is that we often reduce the Bible to our subjective interests. "What does it say to me?" We end up making the text say whatever we want it to say, and as a result, we're doomed to having as many interpretations of the text as there are interpreters. Ironically, while we espouse commitment to the absolute authority of the Word, we often disregard the original intent and "refashion the text in our own image."[3]

So if the Bible is not mainly a rule book or a manual for Christian living, what is it? It's about God and God's glory. It's about God freeing us to live as we were intended to live and the story of all creation being made new. The Scriptures are meant to draw me to the authority of Jesus in my life first and foremost. My understanding of the Bible is always shaped by my prior assumptions—my culture, my upbringing, my experiences, and more. That doesn't mean the Bible is merely subject to what I want it to be, but it does mean I always see it through my thwarted and limited perspective. However, as I begin to view the Bible most as the overarching story by which all other stories make sense, I begin to gain perspective, meaning, and hope. We're invited to continue the story of God as the people who have been called by God to be God's agents in the world. Our story is "the story of God's redeeming presence as narrated in and through the Scriptures."[4] What a source of identity!

How does our view of Scripture influence our cross-cultural practice? Short-term missions projects often include teaching the Bible in some way. Whether it's communicating the gospel with people on the street, teaching children in vacation Bible schools, preaching in churches, or training a group of leaders, we're often put in places where we reference the Bible. Seeing the Bible differently doesn't mean we toss it aside. It simply means we begin to see the assumptions behind our reading and teaching of the Bible.

The Danger of "Biblical" Models

We become most susceptible to the downfalls of misusing the Bible cross-culturally when we teach "biblical" models for ministry. It's not that models based on "successful" churches or individual personalities are better. Clearly, the Bible is a good starting point. But it's dangerous to use our interpretation of the Bible and our experience as proof-texts for how everyone should do ministry. We must beware of arrogantly thinking we can organize the global church around some strategy we're convinced is "biblical," when it may be in fact yet another cultural model.

I spent several years working with a ministry that claimed, "We teach timeless, transferable principles; therefore, our biblical strategy applies worldwide, whatever the context." The problem is that as we sought to implement our biblical strategy in Africa, African leaders insisted on some necessary adjustments to "Jesus's strategy." The same thing happened in India, Brazil, Korea, and the UK. Many recipients of the training weren't convinced this was the timeless, transferable strategy of Jesus. Was it a helpful framework for ministry? Sure. Did it reflect some of the passions and priorities of Jesus? Definitely! Was it Jesus's strategy for how everyone should do ministry in all times and places? Not really.

One day one of our North American trainers said to me, "Look. The same plan Jesus used two thousand years ago is the same plan we must use today. That's the beauty of our training philosophy. It works everywhere. Don't tell me it doesn't work in your context. You have to make it work. Jesus said so."

This stems from the North American church's longtime practice of reading the Gospels as if they were given to us so that we could mimic what Jesus did in the first century. John 20:21 is often used as the proof-text for copying Jesus's ministry. "As the Father has sent me, I am sending you." But to use that isolated verse as fodder to mimic Jesus's ministry one for one is dangerous. Jesus's ministry was geared specifically toward Israel. He came to act out the presence of Yahweh in Israel's very specific story. What God did through Jesus the Messiah was unique and climactic. So when we simply reduce Jesus's ministry to a strategy for how we should do ministry, we run the risk of reducing the importance of the cross and the resurrection, when God defeated the powers of evil and dealt with the sin of the world once and for all.[5]

This doesn't mean Jesus's ministry is irrelevant for us today. But we must grow in our understanding of the historical Jesus within the first-century Palestinian world so that we can follow Jesus more faithfully in our twenty-first-century world. We have to see more clearly who he was and how he responded to the realities of his cultural context as well as his unique mission and then seek to live out that heartbeat in the contexts where we serve.

For example, when we use Jesus as a model for leadership, we have to understand the world in which he led—a world in which Rome was in control, Herod reigned, John was beheaded, Jewish messianic movements were dreamed and schemed, and Jesus preached the Good News of the kingdom. There in the dust and drama of ancient Israel I discover the essence of what it means to embody Jesus in the cultural contexts where I lead. The convictions that drove him then and there give me the resources I need to be a faithful follower and leader here and now. However, I can't simply resort to trying to mimic what Jesus did as a leader. Christ developed his ministry priorities in light of his cultural context. He didn't import a ministry strategy from another culture and force it into the first-century world of Palestine. He didn't take principles developed in one place and try to implement them in another.[6]

Others try too hard to set up the early church in Acts as *the* biblical model. Many attempts have been made to offer transcendent blueprints for church based on what we know of the first-century church. However, the first-century church took on a variety of forms as it expanded to different cultures, and diversity was the norm. Those who wish to get back to the New Testament church, because it was somehow better, need to know there was no single model for the church in the first century.[7] Churches with a Jewish background—such as those in Jerusalem and Antioch—differed considerably from certain churches in the Greco-Roman world, such as those in Ephesus, Corinth, and Rome.

Now clearly the New Testament provides us with some direction for how we should go about living *our* part of God's story. Jesus gives us glimpses of what it looks like to live as we were intended to live in a very specific time and place. The early church gives us a tangible picture of what it looks like for God to continue living on earth through his body—the church—in a variety of cultural contexts. But we must not force a strategy developed for another time and place into our contexts, much less another cross-cultural ministry context. Instead, we must discover the consistent patterns for ministry that surface throughout the story of God and find out what those look like in thousands of cultures around the world.[8]

We elevate the Bible when we seek to understand the life experiences and cultural settings of biblical authors and characters. That in turn helps us to discern what it looks like to live out God's presence in different cultural settings today.

A Multicultural View of the Bible

One of the greatest benefits from traveling to another part of the world is the chance to see the Bible through the eyes of God-fearing people in another culture. Whether the story of Joseph is about loyalty to God despite sexual temptation or loyalty to one's family despite mistreatment is only the beginning of what it means to see Scripture through a multicultural lens.

The Global God[9] is a collection of essays from evangelical scholars around the world. Each scholar describes the attribute of God that is most evident in their respective culture. For example, Dieumeme Noelliste of Haiti describes the emphasis that the Afro-Caribbean Christian church places on the transcendence of God—that is, the infinite ways God is different from us as humans. In contrast, many of our American worship songs emphasize God's immanence—the close, intimate relationship we can have with God and the ways God is like us. Noelliste believes the global church has much to learn from Caribbean believers' understanding of the unspeakable, unfathomable, mysterious holiness of God—God's transcendence.

In contrast, Tsu-Kung Chuang reveals that the Chinese people really don't see the point in separating God's character into transcendent and immanent qualities. Chinese thought has always embraced a continuous unity between the supernatural and the natural. They look for the "sacred" in the "secular" and the "secular" in the "sacred." As a result, Chinese Christians have little difficulty embracing a God who is simultaneously like us and unlike us. They don't see much value in the artificial categories of God's transcendence and immanence.

As a North American, I think transcendence and immanence are extremely helpful ways for me to understand God. I need to embrace the tension of a God who is both from above and right here. However, consider what could happen if I dogmatically taught the principles of transcendence and immanence to a group of Chinese believers. The principles aren't necessarily ones they even need to hold and could in fact detract from their cultural understanding of God. Through dialogue, however, they could learn why I see the need to look at both expressions of God separately, just as I could grow from hearing them describe the continuity of the yin and yang of God's character.

God is not whatever each culture wants to make God be. Instead, our cultural perspectives both limit and enhance our understanding of who God is. My cultural perspective, by itself, gives me a very limited view of the supreme Creator of the universe. However, as I intersect my growing understanding of God's immanence with my Jamaican sister's growing understanding of God's transcendence with my Chinese brother's growing understanding of the amazing unity within the mysterious person of God, we gain a more accurate picture of God than any of us has apart.

This is why assuming we can simply pick and choose biblical principles to dogmatically share with people cross-culturally is filled with problems. Notice the contrast between these North Americans' perspectives on the "biblical" material they taught cross-culturally and the perspective of the majority world church pastors who received the training. The North American pastors and trainers said:

- "We came here to teach about the life of Christ and how he did ministry. So cultural differences really don't matter."
- "I got really frustrated with [the missionary] today when he kept saying, 'There are many different ways you can approach working with youth.' This is not just one of many good approaches. *This is how Jesus did it.*"
- "At first I was stressed in thinking about 'What does ministry look like here?' . . . Then I took a deep breath and remembered all we're teaching are biblical principles, and as long as we stick to those, they're cross-cultural."

- "It's so cool to think that the principles we're teaching are totally transferable for anywhere in the world. Any church, any ministry. It works. It's biblical."

I sat with the majority world church leaders who listened to the trainers who made these statements. After multiple encounters with them and many gracious comments on their part about the trainers, they began to say the following kinds of things in assessing the training they received:

- "In some ways, he described a different Jesus than the one we know. I'm not sure what to do with that."
- "I was surprised we studied Jesus's ministry without really considering any of his miracles and his battling against the supernatural."
- "He kept saying that the primary principle from Jesus's ministry was that he started with a small group and grew a large following. That seems like a very American way of looking at it though. Everything always has to be bigger and better. One of the things we find especially freeing about Jesus's ministry is that it seems his following kept getting smaller and smaller the closer he got to the end."
- "I really enjoyed the materials on how to make our ministry healthy. But why do you think we didn't look at the subject of persecution at all? That seems inconsistent with how God has grown the gospel."
- "I really like the structure. It's good. But I don't think it's the only biblical way to do ministry."
- "I have never met anyone more insensitive to a local culture than this American trainer. . . . I even told him he is terminally offensive in our culture. He said he is transcultural and that he is not American but *biblical* in his values."

It would be unfair to suggest that the training had no value. On the other hand, a realistic perspective will help us look at what is truly biblical in our teaching and what are merely programs and emphases shaped by our cultural contexts. The typical response to conflicting cultural perspectives on the Bible is to try to strip away anything that is cultural, which is of course impossible. Regardless, cross-cultural trainers often attempt to overcome the cultural bias in their teaching by avoiding the use of any illustrations. Recipients ask for the opposite. They don't find purely conceptual material devoid of any examples very helpful. Sharing from our culturally based ministries can be helpful as long as we're careful not to "overbiblicize" them as being the only way to minister.

In addition, there *is* a place for principles. Principles can express the bullets of a larger assumed story. That's not all bad. In fact, it's essential because we can never give a comprehensive account of how our particular topic connects with the entire story of God. We just need to realize that principles, much as single passages of Scripture, are always inadequate at giving the full picture. They help provide a structure by which to communicate truth, but we must never contend that they are the best way to express what needs to be done and understood by everyone everywhere.

Concluding Thoughts

A few weeks ago I was presenting this material to a group of leaders when a hand shot up and an impassioned pastor started shouting at me, "How do you argue with the Bible?! If the Bible isn't cross-cultural then we have a more basic problem. We've moved out of the realm of orthodoxy!"

I tried to defuse his emotions by suggesting I wasn't interested in arguing with the Bible. I'm interested in questioning who decides which principles of the Bible are truly transcultural and how we extrapolate those principles devoid of culture.

God's redemptive story applies to every tribe, nation, and tongue. However, our understanding of God's Word is always skewed by our cultural context, and at the very least, our cultural biases need to be acknowledged up front when teaching from the Word at any time, but especially overseas. My perceptions of Jesus are filled with twenty-first-century Western assumptions. I need to gain a more accurate first-century picture of Jesus so I can do the hard work of understanding how to follow him and describe him in the twenty-first century.

There is only one Jesus and only one Bible that records his words. Differences lie in the assumptions we bring to studying Jesus and his Word. We must always leave our perceptions of who he is subject to correction. The Christian message is truly universal in scope. "The truth is becoming ever-more apparent . . . that Jesus is at home nowhere in this world, yet everywhere."[10]

7

Money

"They're So Happy"

Through the eyes of North Americans . . .	Through the eyes of majority world Christians . . .
We who were born in America have to understand, we hit the lottery by growing up here.[1]	Why do they think we're so poor? What makes them think we want what they have?

Our family lived in Singapore for a while. After being there for a few weeks, Linda and I decided it was time for our girls to encounter a little broader experience of Asia. We wanted them to taste and see something other than Singapore's slick, modernized streets lined with countless Starbucks and trendy shopping centers. So we crossed the Straits of Johor and entered the world of Malaysia. Within our first few minutes in the developing world of Malaysia, we experienced a much rawer, edgier atmosphere. We were solicited for money and walked by a leper. We noticed that less attention seemed to be given to covering up the good and the bad of life and society. I was totally energized. I love robust, authentic places like Johor. And I was excited about the chance for our family to get a taste of a place that much more closely resembles where much of the world lives than either Singapore or Midwest America.

Prior to our trip to Malaysia, we'd told our girls to each pick out a toy they could give to a child in Malaysia. We described for them the poverty of many of the children in places like Malaysia. Emily, my older daughter, picked out a stuffed frog, and Grace chose some candy to give away. Clearly, these weren't very "sacrificial gifts," but we were going to start small with instilling in them a spirit of generosity. The girls were excited to embark on a "short-term mission" of their own.

Not too long into our day trip, it started to rain. We were stranded under a covered walkway for a while. I looked around me and saw a Malay man with his daughter. They were passing time sitting in the dirt, and they looked like prime targets for our "planned generosity." I leaned over to Emily and said, "See that little girl over there. I bet she would love the frog you brought. Let's go take it to her." Wide-eyed, Emily and I walked over to the little girl, tried to communicate nonverbally a bit, and handed her the stuffed frog. The little girl hugged it and held it close to her. After a few minutes of smiling back and forth, we didn't know what else to do so we smiled and started to walk away. As we started to leave, the dad ordered his daughter to return the frog. We motioned that we didn't want it back, but he insisted. He began to raise his voice and grabbed the frog and handed it to me. I tried once more to express that we wanted her to have it, but he wouldn't hear of it.

I walked away a little frustrated that my daughter's first experience with giving to the developing world wasn't going quite the way I had hoped. We eventually found some kids who took our girls' gifts, but it wasn't nearly as easy to give our stuff away as we'd thought it would be. As I began to talk with Linda about it, we thought back to our home in the Chicago area. Though we had a very nice house, our home was one of the more modest ones in our neighborhood. Linda asked me, "So how would you feel if one of the parents in the million-dollar homes near us suddenly walked up to our girls and started handing them gifts?" All of a sudden I began to see this in a new light. If some rich person started giving my girls unsolicited gifts in my presence, I'd think, *I'm quite capable of caring for them myself, thank you!*

The last thing I want to imply is that we should keep our things to ourselves so as not to insult people by our generosity. However, dealing with people who live with a very different level of financial resources is complex. Generosity brings with it subtle, important issues related to power. We need to widen our perspective to think about how to respond to the poverty we often encounter when we travel to new cultural contexts. We want to explore the "power of generosity" through three questions: Who's "poor"? Who decides what the needs are? and To give or not to give?

Who's "Poor"?

One time I watched a Diane Sawyer interview with Brad Pitt. I was interested to hear how he would talk about his involvement in the One campaign (www.one.org), a global initiative to reduce poverty. The mantras of the One campaign are as follows: "*One* billion people live on less than *one* dollar a day. *One* by *one*, we can help them help themselves." I'm glad to join a collective voice that calls each of us to consider what we can do to respond to poverty. The goals are ambitious—to cut global poverty in half by 2015 and to rid the world of extreme poverty by 2025.

Regardless of how you feel about the government getting involved in reducing global poverty, Pitt's participation is inspiring. He told Sawyer, "I can't get out of the press. These [Africans] can't get in the press. So let's redirect the attention a little bit. It drives me mental seeing what I've seen and knowing that it doesn't show up in our news every day. I mean, literally thousands of people died today!"

Amid his good intentions, however, he kept saying, "Listen, we who were born in America have to understand, we hit the lottery by growing up here, by being born here."[2] Pitt commiserates with poor Africans who didn't get to be born in the land of the red, white, and blue. I don't want to undermine someone from Hollywood speaking to a good cause. Thank God for that! Frankly, the church could take some cues from people like Pitt who are casting a vision for something so noble. Pitt's lottery-winning sentiment, however, is one of the troubling comments I hear from short-termers as they return from the developing world. We come home talking about how blessed we are to live in North America. There are huge privileges that come with being born in certain parts of the world. However, are we implying that those not born in North America *aren't* blessed? We must resist thinking that everyone longs to live here. There are privileges that come with being African and Chinese and Latin. There are blessings inherent to people living in places all over the world. We need to realize that not everyone in the world longingly wishes they had been born as a North American.

Not all Africans are starving and waiting for heroic Westerners to come and save them. People in places like Ethiopia, Ghana, and Uganda are grateful for the money raised through efforts such as the One campaign but hate the idea that the world still sees Africa as a place "where nothing ever grows, no rain nor rivers flow," as sung in Bob Geldof's twenty-year-old hit, "Do They Know It's Christmas?" The message of Ethiopia as a starving, helpless country has so per-meated people's thinking that Ethiopian tourist agencies often field inquiries from travelers who wonder if there will be any food available for them to eat when they arrive in Addis Ababa.

While the poverty, illiteracy, and disease throughout Africa are devastating, Africa is also a place where many people are *not* starving. Democracy has begun to take hold in many of its nations, and Africans currently grapple with answers to their own problems. More than 90 percent of Africans surveyed by a BBC poll said they are proud to be African.[3] They don't feel like they lost the lottery!

Many short-term missions endeavors force us to face the issue of poverty head-on. My friend Ashish came from northern India to visit me in Chicago a few years ago. We were eating at Gino's Pizzeria one day and ran into a youth pastor I knew, along with his youth group. They had just returned from Central America and were spending a day in Chicago to debrief their trip. Ashish asked the group, "So what did you learn from your trip?" Student after student obsessed about the poverty of "those poor people."

After the youth group left, Ashish said to me, "Why do they think we're so poor? What makes them think we want what they have?" Sipping my third refill, I retorted, "Ashish. Give me a break! This is a good thing. Financially speaking you *are* poor compared to any of those kids. It's so hard to get their minds off their consumerist passions. I'm really grateful to hear they experienced some dissonance when they saw the poverty."

Ashish rebutted, "Well, that's nice and all, but I'm so sick of sympathetic Westerners who think we need more stuff. Why would that have anything to do with our happiness? Please don't import the idol of consumerism into India." He went on to tell me about the North American group who was just with him in Delhi. "They were really concerned about the bicycle I used to get back and forth to church," he said. "They found out how 'inexpensively' they could purchase me a car, and without even asking me, they informed me they had all chipped in to get me a little car! The last thing I wanted was a car. I had to find a tactful way of telling them that if they really wanted to invest in something, I had several members in my church who could use those same dollars to help set up a microenterprise development. But I think I kind of 'rained on their parade' as you say. They thought I was just being super-sacrificial."

Granted, some Indians would have jumped at the chance to receive a car from a well-intentioned short-term missions team, and some Africans wish they had been born in North America. And the last thing I want to do is diminish the importance of giving sacrificially and generously. We need to do that. But as with all the other realities we've been encountering on this journey together, meeting the needs of others requires us to question our assumptions before acting. We need to serve with eyes wide open and understand that there are ways we're poor and ways we're rich. The same is true in the majority world.

In our attempts to be generous, we presume others want what we have to give them. Worse yet, sometimes we're the first ones to tell the majority world that they're poor. One Ugandan church leader said it this way: "We did not know we were poor until someone from the outside told us."[4]

Who Decides What the Needs Are?

One of the things that drove me to write this book was my concern that short-term missions participants might continue to make the same mistakes made by mission workers in the past. The assumption that we know what is most needed by people in another place is the assumption that allowed Rome, England, and Spain to say their colonialist domination was not primarily self-centered. Our financial wealth, and all the amenities that accompany it, easily inclines us to think we know what other people need.

I often participate in conferences where short-term missions agencies have exhibits. When I ask an organization's representative how the majority church is engaged in what they're doing overseas, I often hear, "Oh yes, we're very committed to working with the national churches there. We ask them if they want to be involved." Did you catch that? We ask them if *they* want to be involved. Maybe we should start by asking if *we* should be involved at all, and if so, how? What might it look like if on-the-ground ministry leaders helped us open our eyes to the real needs? Not only is it colonialist to invite locals' input on the back end of planning, but we often end up doing irrelevant and costly work. Local ownership means more than inviting participation or asking for input. It means letting the local churches actually direct and shape what we do in our cross-cultural efforts; they ask *us* if we want to be involved rather than vice versa.

Building projects are one of the most popular kinds of short-term missions endeavors—building churches, rebuilding homes after a natural disaster, building ministry centers, and so on. I've done my share of mixing cement, painting walls, and nailing in studs. Believe me, if you knew my total ineptness at any kind of home-improvement project, you'd get a good laugh thinking about me trying to put a roof on a church building in South America.

How do the locals feel about our building pursuits on "their" behalf? As with most of these issues, the reviews are mixed. Many express gratitude at seeing fair-skinned kids give up two weeks of vacation to sweat it out as they mix cement all day long a world away from their backyard swimming pools. We've all watched the video testimonials about how life is completely different now because of the homes built, the hospital maintenance that took place, and the brand-new roof on the church.

Others struggle with the thought of how many locals could be employed by investing the money spent on a typical short-term building project. Local ministries see short-term groups raise money for a one-week trip that exceeds a majority world church's annual budget.

Jo Ann Van Engen, a missionary in Honduras, contends, "Short-term mission groups almost always do work that could be done (and usually done better) by people of the country they visit. The spring-break group spent their time and money painting and cleaning the orphanage in Honduras. That money could have paid two Honduran painters who desperately needed the work, with enough left over to hire four new teachers, build a new dormitory, and provide each child with new clothes."[5]

One Honduran bricklayer had this to say about his experience working with a building team: "I found out soon enough that I was in the way. The group wanted to do things their way and made me feel like I didn't know what I was doing. I only helped the first day."[6]

A ministry leader in Zimbabwe asks us to remember that Africans also know how to build buildings. In talking about one of the groups that visited his community, he said, "It isn't that they didn't work hard. . . . But they must remember that we built buildings before they came, and we will build buildings after they leave. Unfortunately, while they were here, they thought they were the only ones who knew how to build buildings."[7]

Is it wrong to build buildings? Some think so, but I think there can be a place for it. But we must plan these efforts with an understanding about the true needs, how we can help meet those needs, and how to use an approach that is helpful for the long haul. We *do* have something to offer, but let's discover what that is through dialogue with the majority world church.

A group from my church just returned from a couple weeks in Rwanda. Within their first hour in Rwanda, the local team said, "Ninety percent of your job is done. You're here. Your presence speaks volumes." One of the team members told me she thought, "Well, I don't think so. That's gracious of you, but we're here to work hard." The longer she was there, however, the more she began to see that the tasks they had gone to do were not what was needed most. Their presence and the chance for relationships seemed to be more press-ing needs for the Rwandan church than any menial tasks that were planned. Do the menial tasks; they teach us about serving, and we get to serve alongside our brothers and sisters. Be sure to remember, however, that painting a room for our brothers and sisters or putting in windows isn't really what it's about. It's about meeting a deeper need in us and in them.

These issues aren't exclusive to short-term missions work done overseas. I recently talked with an African-American pastor from Cincinnati who said he gets an average of ten phone calls a day at Christmastime from local pastors who want to donate clothes and toys. As much as he appreciates the goodwill, he says, "No thanks. What we really need are people willing to build relationships with many of our single moms. We need tutors for kids. We need people who can invite folks over for dinner and vice versa." The pastor went on to tell me, "After hundreds of conversations like that over the last five years, only one church has taken me up on my counteroffer."

Shane Claiborne of the Simple Way in Philadelphia thinks most North American Christians do care about the poor. He says, "I believe the great tragedy of the church is not that rich Christians do not *care* about the poor, but that they do not *know* the poor."[8] He believes we resort to charitable giving as a way to ease our consciences rather than really entering into mutually enriching relationships with people who are financially poor.

To Give or Not to Give?

If we think of people as "poor," we demean them. If we ignore the fact that two billion people live on less than two dollars a day, we're selfish consumers. Is there any way out of this?

This is precisely the dilemma Boone, from Richard Dooling's *White Man's Grave*, was feeling as he continued to experience life as an American in the world of Sierra Leone. Boone refused to be the rich North American who had African servants working for him while he looked for his Peace Corps friend Michael. Boone turned down six kids who wanted to be his servants. His African host says, "You're a millionaire. Share the wealth. For 25 cents, someone will clean your room. For a dime, someone will walk 2 miles for you to get a bucket of water for you to bathe in. Nobody here is going to admire you for not hiring servants. You'll just be thought of as unbelievably stingy."[9]

This example brings up the same kind of dissonance I feel when I'm told I shouldn't give money to homeless people because they'll just spend it on more alcohol. But the alternative, avoiding eye contact and ignoring a person in need, doesn't sit right. There is a clear ethical responsibility that comes with encountering poverty.[10]

Terence Linhart talks about how encountering poverty challenged the high school students from Indiana who traveled to Ecuador. Eighteen-year-old Amy looked over the town from her hotel and said, "It's just amazing, the poverty. Like, it breaks my heart, but it makes me feel so spoiled, and like I'm such an evil person."[11] Another student said, "Living in America is a blessing and a curse at the same time. There's a blessing because you have all this stuff, but all the stuff is a curse, you know?"[12]

Adults report the same kind of dilemma when returning from short-term missions trips. Typical comments made by adult participants include: "We're so blessed. I realize it when I see how little they have." "I'm so encouraged by how much they do with so little." "I have it so good and I never want to take it for granted after seeing the joy in these people's faces even though they have so little." My fear is that this kind of observation makes it too easy to jump on a plane in Ecuador or Ethiopia and go home convinced that "those people are so happy just the way they are!"

On the other hand, many people living in poverty possess amazing wealth in other areas. Rather than demeaning them as tragic objects to be rescued, we need to see them as our equals so we can walk with them and learn from them, each benefiting from one another's "wealth" and sacrifice.[13]

Concluding Thoughts

The realities that come with money cause me a great deal of personal dissonance. Even as I write, I'm doing so from the cozy Starbucks a few blocks from my home. I'm well aware of the many whose weekly wage is equal to the cost of the latte I'm sipping. That's problematic, but how might our sympathy for fellow brothers and sisters in Christ in majority world places lead us to treat them in demeaning ways? Our wealth creates all kinds of power issues, and as much as we want to talk about collaborative relationships between churches in different cultures, a majority world church leader who feels safe to be really honest with you may well confess that he realizes the need to keep the "partnering" church in the West happy so that funds keep flowing.

On the other hand, we must not ease our consciences by thinking they're happy enough without our money. Maybe I need to sip a few less lattes every week and invest those same dollars to help free a couple young girls in Bangkok from prostitution. What if we committed to spend at least as much money supporting the projects we visit on our short-term trips as we do on getting us there? What if our building projects included hiring local labor and only buying local materials?

The road forward requires us to look at some of these tensions. As we look honestly at the complexity of the issues related to money, our perspective begins to widen, which allows us to serve more effectively. All this perspective widening will translate into action. Changed perspective equals changed practice. We'll look at that more in part 3, but first we need to look at one more reality in North American short-term missions. This one overrides all the others.

8

Simplicity

"You're Either for Us or against Us!"

Through the eyes of North Americans . . .	Through the eyes of majority world Christians . . .
It was unbelievable. They treated us like rock stars. The Brazilians were like storming the stage, asking for our autographs, and chasing our buses. I don't think they get to see Americans very often.	This was all a big joke one of our Brazilian friends started. We pretended they were famous by storming the stage and asking for their autographs. But we live in Sao Paulo—one of the most cosmopolitan cities in the world. We've seen plenty of Americans.

President George W. Bush will be chronicled in history books for his frequently repeated mantra to the world, "You're either with us or you're for the terrorists."[1]

Many of my friends from other parts of the world were confused by his statement and, even more, the thinking behind it. Shortly after 9/11, one of my Asian friends said to me, "I don't for a second condone what the terrorists did to you on 9/11. It was a horrifying time for all of us to see you attacked that way. So I'm not for the terrorists. But neither can I support the way the US so quickly moved into Iraq and Afghanistan without more global input. Why does it have to be an either/or?"

Filmmaker Michael Moore appears to exercise the same kind of either/or oversimplification for which he so brutally attacks Bush in his documentary film *Fahrenheit 9/11*. Moore asked Pete Townshend, British rock star of The Who, for permission to use his anthem "Won't Get Fooled Again" as part of the soundtrack for *Fahrenheit 9/11*. Townshend refused because he felt that Moore's previous works demonstrated bullying and a lack of critical engagement with key issues. In response, Moore accused Townshend of being a war supporter. Townshend said Moore's attitude seemed like the very credo he was criticizing in Bush: "If you're not with me, you're against me."[2]

I'm not after a political debate right now. I'm more interested in looking at the very American-like simplicity demonstrated by Bush and Moore alike. The simplicity conflict cuts across all the other factors we've considered. Our conclusions about why we should go, our sense of urgency, and our use of Scripture and money all flow from our tendency to oversimplify complex issues. In particular, the quest to find common ground is seamlessly related to the simplicity conflict.

Simplistic categories have been central to our US ethos. An American is either Republican or Democrat, blue collar or white collar, liberal or conservative, modern or postmodern, environmentalist or industrialist. Of course, one of the things that's happened in our twenty-first-century world is an exposure of the fallacy of these clear-cut categories. Life isn't that neatly ordered. There is a place for simplicity. A few things in life are clear-cut, but most of life is not. In particular, most cross-cultural issues are far too complex to be placed in one category or another. The simplicity factor shows up in short-term missions through an overuse of the K.I.S.S. principle, the rock-star complex, and the ways short-term missionaries describe the lessons they learned.

The K.I.S.S. Principle

North American Christians have often embraced the K.I.S.S. (Keep It Simple, Stupid) principle for many purposes. K.I.S.S. is a familiar mantra in short-term missions too, whether it's the importance of simplicity in planning our itinerary, our testimony, or our plans for follow-up. "Keep it simple," we're told.

There *is* a place for the K.I.S.S. principle. I spend a great deal of time in university settings, where we often make things unnecessarily complicated. Overcomplexity can paralyze us and keep us from getting anywhere. But many times K.I.S.S. becomes a hindrance to cultural intelligence. If we overemphasize the K.I.S.S. principle and never ask the deeper questions, we're at risk of missing some core issues, particularly in cross-cultural work. We'll keep it simple but remain stupid.

We already looked at how easily we inaccurately interpret familiar behaviors. Short-termers assume smiling, nodding, and silence mean the same things for all people. Likewise, the way we too quickly apply the behavior of one person to everyone in a culture is another demonstration of the K.I.S.S. principle negatively at work.

I first became aware of the prevalence of the K.I.S.S. principle in short-term work when I began asking short-term participants what they observed about the new context they visited. When I asked, "What's the number one thing that stands out in your mind from what you experienced in this new cultural context?" I most often heard these kinds of responses, from both adults and youth:

- "People were driving on the wrong side of the road. That was the first thing I noticed, as well as the foreign language of course, and having to figure out their money."
- "I always notice the children most. I never get used to seeing these young kids have to beg for food. It's so unfair that kids have to grow up there."
- "It's not as modern as things here. They don't have jetways at the airports, and they aren't very organized."
- "The buildings and cars are different. . . . They don't have standards for that kind of stuff like we do."
- "The poverty is what I notice the most. It's hard to believe people live in conditions like that. And they have chain-link fences everywhere."
- "I just notice how happy everyone is. They have so little but they're so happy."

By now, you probably recognize many of these kinds of statements from the last several chapters. One of the things I'm striving for in

this book is to help us move away from using the K.I.S.S. principle
as our guiding protocol for short-term work. Lumping everything
into simplistic categories or looking at only surface-level issues is
not helpful in bringing about effective ministry across cultures. You
don't need a graduate course in intercultural studies to do short-term
missions well. However, we have to open our eyes to some of the
things happening below the surface. We'll look at some suggestions
on how to get there in the next section. Before we get there, though,
let's look at a couple of the other ways we tend to oversimplify our
thinking in short-term missions.

The Rock-Star Complex

Another way the simplicity factor frequently shows up is through the
presence of a rock-star complex when we serve cross-culturally for a
few days. This is another way to describe ethnocentrism—the tendency
to define what's normal and best based on our own cultural perspective. It's the assumption that the world revolves around us. Here are
a couple ways I've seen ethnocentrism or the rock-star complex get
played out on short-term trips.

A few years ago, I attended a church service in the Chicago area
in which a youth group was reporting on its recent two-week trip to
Sao Paulo, Brazil. The youth group had done a number of musical
and dramatic presentations in public schools, churches, and shopping
centers throughout Sao Paulo. The team of students and adults described the typical things heard from a group like this, including the
ways their hearts were stretched by the generosity and contentment
of the people, the challenge to consider missions as a vocation, and
the need for us to pray for the struggling, small Brazilian churches.

In addition, nearly every student described how strange it was
to be treated like rock stars whenever they completed one of their
performances. One student said, "It was unbelievable. They treated
us like rock stars. The Brazilians were like storming the stage, asking
for our autographs, and chasing our buses as we drove away. I don't
think they get to see Americans very often."

That same night, I met a couple Brazilian teenagers who had been
with this youth group in Sao Paulo and were now in the US for a

year as exchange students. Given my interest in comparing North American perceptions of short-term missions with those of the people who receive them, I asked them what they observed about the North American group while they were there. The Brazilian teenagers spoke warmly of the friendships they developed, particularly since they themselves were now on the other side of cross-cultural travel. They talked about the joy they experienced as they heard the testimonies and music from these American students.

After the Brazilian students spent a lot of time affirming the Chicago students, I jumped in and said, "So tell me about this whole thing of being treated like rock stars." The Brazilian students immediately started laughing and blushing. After I insisted they tell me what was so funny, they said, "Okay—this is so bad. But this was all a big joke one of our Brazilian friends started. He decided we'd make them think they were famous and everything by storming the stage, asking for their autographs, getting their pictures, and that kind of stuff. I mean, we live in Sao Paulo—one of the most cosmopolitan cities in the world. We've seen plenty of Americans. Don't get me wrong. We enjoyed their music and drama and stuff, but they weren't exactly 'rock stars' in our eyes."

You certainly can't fault the North American students for being confused. They were duped. But the problem was when they jumped to a conclusion about what this all meant. And before we're too quick to explain this away as youthful naïveté, I haven't seen a significant difference among adults who go overseas on short-term trips. The rock-star complex is the same tendency that drove the North American pastors to confidently claim, "They're so hungry for our training" and "We have a biblical model that applies to everyone."

Some people have said to me, "C'mon. This rock-star syndrome isn't unique to cross-cultural ministry. This is just arrogance. That's why these kids think everyone wants their autographs. That's why pastors assume everyone wants their training."

I'm not so sure! Certainly, all of us struggle with wanting to prove ourselves. So I'm sure some of that weaves through our cross-cultural behaviors. But I think this is more than pride.

One of the things that surprised me most in my study of North American pastors' cross-cultural training was the difference between what they said before they went on their trips and how they behaved when they got there. In my conversations with them prior to their trips, they espoused and demonstrated a strong spirit of humility. They weren't the self-absorbed people they may appear to be when we read their arrogant, insensitive comments written on a page. Likewise, most of the high school students I talk to about their mission trips are conscious of wanting to be learners. So why do they still end up being so ethnocentric and colonialist in their cross-cultural work? Why do they develop a rock-star complex? In part, it comes back to the issue of simplicity.

On the whole, North Americans are not inclined to reflective thinking beyond surface-level observations. The K.I.S.S. principle drives much of how we approach cross-cultural work, so the rock-star syndrome is an inevitable result. By failing to look at the deeper issues, we come to false conclusions. My concern is not so much that a group of teenagers didn't catch on to what was happening. My concern is that the rock-star complex reveals another way that our perspective influences the ways we engage with people as we relate and serve.

Takeaways

One more way the simplicity factor is blatantly evident in a lot of short-term missions work is that we repeat, with amazing regularity, the same takeaways from these trips. It's as if we've been scripted with the right answers for what we learned from a trip. We parrot one another with statements such as these:

"We have it so good here."

"We're so caught up in materialism."

"We need to pray more."

"I felt so close to God there. He's doing amazing things there."

With little variation, these are the things reported in follow-up letters and given in testimonials. When I asked Rhonda, a thirty-year-old woman, how her experience in Africa changed her, she said, "We have so much, and they have so little. That's a plus for us because we're so blessed. I mean, we all have running water, electricity, telephones, computers, and cars that go down the street with no problem. And the power doesn't go out. . . . But our material possessions can be a hindrance because they keep us from really focusing on God."

Bill, a fifty-two-year-old pastor from Southern California, said, "I was really encouraged to see how they deal with so little and how strong their faith is. That makes my needs in life and ministry seem so small comparatively, or at least different."

Shannon, a twenty-seven-year-old woman, said, "I never want to forget some of the things I've seen this last week. These people do so much with so little. I have it so good."

Ken, a thirty-year-old man, said, "The biggest thing I learned was the power of prayer."

These adults' reflections are largely reminiscent of what teenagers have to say about their experiences. Remember Amy's comment: "It's just amazing, the poverty. Like, it breaks my heart, but it makes me feel so spoiled, and like I'm such an evil person."[3] More than two-thirds of the high school students I surveyed about their mission trips said something like fifteen-year-old Ryan: "I just felt so close to God when I was there. I wish I could keep that feeling alive at home, but I know I won't."[4]

In many ways, these are rich, potentially life-changing conclusions. Exposure to what God is doing among other believers around the world, being conscious about our wealth and the trappings thereof, and suspending "life as normal" for a few days as a way to deepen intimacy with God—who can argue with that?

However, one of the more troubling comments I heard from a group of majority world pastors who were giving me their frank perspective on North American short-term trips was this: "You talk about us to your churches back home in such demeaning ways."

I pushed back. "Really? You usually come off as heroes in the reports I hear. You would think your churches were nearly perfect from what most short-termers say about you."

They weren't so sure. Our exaggerations about how locals are so dependent on these short-term teams and the long-term impact of the work, the jokes about the weird foods and the destitute conditions, and the exaggerated reports about what was accomplished often lead our brothers and sisters to feel demeaned.

I'm troubled by the way our simplicity plays out in statements about what happened in our lives as a result of our short-term sojourns. I expected more, particularly out of the adults, and especially the pastors. While we describe the dissonance we feel as we see our wealth juxtaposed against poverty, it seems to have little influence on the number of souvenirs we purchase or the choices we make when we get home. Participants rarely describe a significant change in how they think about God and their faith as a result of trips like these. In fact, rather than being challenged to see Christianity differently, participants talk most about how Christ and his bride are the same everywhere.

All too often, the short-term experience "eludes any significant reflection on the deeper assumptions and attitudes that structure one's view of God, of themselves, and of host strangers."[5] Terence Linhart reports that the Indiana group he studied demonstrated an "absence of theological reflection about their ministry programs they were conducting, no attempts to understand the incongruity between poverty and joy, and no awareness of new experiences that contradicted previous observations or interpretations."[6]

Clearly, some participants experience deep transformation and come home with very different descriptions of what occurred within them. But why aren't there more? Why are our takeaways always the same surface-level things? What can we do to make long-term transformation more common among the millions of North Americans who participate in short-term missions every year?

Concluding Thoughts

Our understanding and thinking about what we experience on short-term missions are often oversimplified. As a result, our expectations and motivations are inaccurate. Our desire to "Just do it" comes from a short-term perspective rather than a long-term vision. Our tendency to look for similarities often keeps us from seeing differences, and as a result we miss out on the more colorful picture that exists among the people of the world. Our reduction of the Bible to manageable concepts and cultural principles sucks the life out of the story of God. Our simplistic approaches to help poor people end up exposing our own poverty. Simplicity is endemic to short-term missions. It's part of what it means to be an American. It's part of what it means to be a North American evangelical. But it doesn't have to be.

There's an endearing simplicity to Jesus's focus as he goes about his ministry. Yet a quick perusal of his use of parables and his upside-down approach to challenging the established religious system ought to warn any of us against labeling Jesus the epitome of simplicity. Our response should not be to see how complicated we can make short-term missions. Instead, we must acknowledge that we shouldn't be content simply to look at what we can see with a quick glance. We've been on a journey to open our eyes wider in order to see what we may have missed before. Are you beginning to see it? Is your vision broadening?

PART 3

Sharpening Our Focus and Service with Cultural Intelligence (CQ)

What should we make of all this? Should we throw up our hands in despair, cut up our passports, and throw out every letter soliciting funds for short-term missions? Believe me, there have been times when I was ready to go there. Countless pages in my journals from the last several years contain entries like this one:

> Is all the money and effort invested in short-term work paying off? As short-termers, we're often ill-equipped to solve the real needs that exist in the places we visit. Locals are enduring our water bottles and weak stomachs, and we're spending millions of dollars to do it. Is there a way to truly make short-term missions a win-win?

At the end of the day, I'm not convinced we're without hope in seeing short-term missions as an effective tool for serving God's church globally. If criticisms alone are enough reason to abandon the entire movement, then let's be consistent. We're not short on criticisms about long-term missions either. Just because there are some challenges and problems doesn't mean we should abandon the whole thing. I'm committed to seeing us redeem short-term missions. How might we engage in short-term missions with eyes wide open and use it as a way to widen our perspective? How can the dollars we invest in short-term missions be stewarded toward long-term transformation of everyone involved? It's time to strive for a more solution-oriented focus: short-term missions with cultural intelligence.

When I began researching short-term missions, I didn't want to be a researcher who simply pointed out problems without offering any solutions. So I reviewed materials and programs that were developed to improve people's cross-cultural effectiveness. I studied many of the training programs designed for missionaries, Peace Corps workers, and others who moved internationally for overseas assignments. I resonated with the emphasis on taking the time to learn the language, customs, and cultural values. But I knew these approaches wouldn't work for most short-term missions teams. As much as I'd love to see every short-term missionary become fluent in the language and customs of the culture they visit, it's simply unrealistic. That's when a friend introduced me to Dr. Soon Ang, a fellow Christian who was pioneering the research on cultural intelligence, or CQ.

Don't be alarmed by the academic sound of CQ. CQ is just a way of measuring and improving the way we interact in different cultures. The theory was developed using some of the same ideas used to develop IQ, EQ, and the theory of multiple intelligences. We're all pretty familiar with the idea of IQ—a way to measure our intellectual capabilities. And many of us are familiar with the idea of EQ, or emotional intelligence—the ability to assess and regulate the emotions of ourselves and others. CQ picks up right where EQ leaves off. It's the ability to adjust how we think and behave in various cultural situations.

CQ is a skill set that can be learned and developed over time, and the materials in this section are a way to begin that process. By the way, you're already on your way. One of the biggest steps toward enhancing your CQ is simply to open your eyes to the realities of the world and to the challenges of cross-cultural interactions—that's what we've spent the last several chapters exploring.

Don't try to attain a perfect CQ score (which doesn't really exist) by the time you go on your next trip. Our desire is simply to use the last section of this book to embark on a lifelong journey of growing in CQ as a way to more effectively love God and others in the twenty-first-century world. CQ will help us sharpen our focus and service in short-term missions, and it can enhance our ability to interact across cultures day in and day out as we move throughout the twenty-first-century world.

CQ consists of four capabilities, all of which are linked together. As demonstrated in figure 1 below, the four capabilities of CQ are:

CQ Drive: Your level of interest, drive, and motivation to adapt cross-culturally.

CQ Knowledge: Your understanding about how cultures are similar and different.

CQ Strategy: Your ability to interpret cues and plan in light of your cultural understanding.

CQ Action: Your ability to behave appropriately when relating and serving cross-culturally.

Figure 1: Four Different CQ Capabilities

Cultural intelligence includes four capabilities (drive, knowledge, strategy, and action), each of which contributes to your overall CQ.

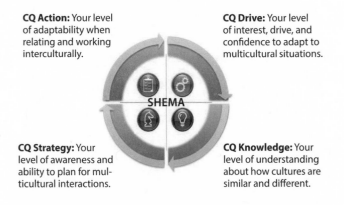

CQ Action: Your level of adaptability when relating and working interculturally.

CQ Drive: Your level of interest, drive, and confidence to adapt to multicultural situations.

CQ Strategy: Your level of awareness and ability to plan for multicultural interactions.

CQ Knowledge: Your level of understanding about how cultures are similar and different.

SHEMA

Most materials designed for short-term work emphasize two of these capabilities: CQ Knowledge (cultural understanding) and CQ Action (cross-cultural behavior). But all four capabilities are needed for effective short-term missions. The interdependence of these four capabilities is important, because having one without the others may actually be worse than having none of them.[1]

You can find information about how to assess your CQ at www.culturalQ.com. This tool is an academically proven way of measuring CQ in all four areas.

The next four chapters describe the four capabilities of CQ. We'll look at a brief explanation of each capability, suggest some ways to nurture growth in each of them, and demonstrate what they look like in real life by going on a journey to Shanghai, China, with a group of college students.[2]

9

Try, Try Again

CQ Drive

ight Christian college students left their dorm rooms in Indiana to spend their January term in Shanghai, China. Members of the team are all TESL (Teaching English as a Second Language) students who by participating in this two-week mission trip will also receive three credits and hands-on experience in TESL. They raised support from family and friends, promoting the trip as a chance to share the gospel with Chinese peers who want to learn English. The team is led by Jake, a senior marketing major with a minor in TESL. Jake grew up as a missionary kid in Mexico. He's spent more time living outside the United States than in it. The group's Chinese host is Tan Jun.

After picking up the American students at the airport, Jun took them to a crowded Shanghai restaurant. Fortunately for the team, Jun speaks flawless English. After they were seated at the restaurant, Jun smiled and said, "Perhaps you're tired after your long journey."

Jake, the team leader, said, "Yeah, we're pretty wasted, but it will be good to eat something other than plane food!"

After dinner, Jun decided the team should take a stroll down Nanjing Road, one of the busiest shopping districts in China. The streets were mobbed with people. The North American students were exhilarated and exhausted all at the same time. The pollution seemed intense, and the noise level caused a major headache for several of the jet-lagged students. Jun bought them all some dumplings at a hawker stall and insisted they try them. Brian, covering his mouth as he yawned, said, "So Jun. Where are we staying tonight? Is it close to here?"

"Don't worry," replied Jun. "We'll go there after a while. I'll show you where it is."

Brian muttered to Sarah, who was walking next to him, "What I'm worried about is getting away from the stench and noise and lying down flat for the first time in thirty-two hours!"

Sarah said, "Remember, Brian, these are things Chinese people always do—stay up late, eat, and shop."

"Well, I'm not Chinese!" Brian said a little louder than he meant to.

Brian is four months away from graduation. He hopes this trip will help him figure out how to use his TESL degree. He's a little annoyed that the next three days are devoted to touring Shanghai because what he really came to do was teach English. As great as it will be to hang out with the rest of the team in Shanghai, Brian didn't come here to eat squishy foods and visit temples. He came to teach English and share the gospel!

The more tired the students became, the less difference their pre-trip orientation seemed to have on their attitudes and behaviors. They were jet-lagged, tired, sweaty, queasy, and way out of their comfort zones. They just wanted to sleep. Finally, when they arrived at the hostel where they were staying, Brian was relieved to see a McDonald's just a block away.

The motivation for participating in short-term missions was the first conflicting image we examined in part 2. Going merely for the sake of adventure or to experience a new place can get in the way of doing short-term missions well. On the other hand, viewing cultural experiences as a distraction from our true mission is equally problematic. The motivation behind our service is the first issue addressed by cultural intelligence: CQ Drive.

What Is CQ Drive?

CQ Drive refers to our level of interest and motivation to adapt cross-culturally. It's a traveler's robustness, courage, hardiness, and capability to persevere through cultural differences. A person high in CQ Drive draws great satisfaction from being in new places and interacting with people from different cultures. A person low in CQ Drive avoids engagement with the culture as a whole. Short-termers with low CQ Drive hope to stay in comfortable hotels, interact primarily with their fellow teammates, and eat familiar foods. In contrast, short-termers with high CQ Drive want to adapt to the new culture not only to do short-term missions well but also because they're genuinely interested in learning about life in a different place.

People high in CQ Drive are internally motivated to learn about a new place. They want to ask the deeper questions that come about best through CQ Strategy, something we'll look at later. As they begin to observe differences and some of the ways their own assumptions are challenged, they don't run from facing those differences. Instead, they persist in trying to adapt in light of their observations. They don't persevere through this process in isolation. They actively seek relationships with people who are culturally different. For these kinds of individuals, a short-term missions trip is just one of many opportunities in the course of a year when they will seek out cross-cultural experiences. A person with high CQ Drive is always on the lookout for opportunities to understand different cultures and different ways of seeing the world.

CQ Drive is one of the most overlooked aspects of short-term missions. CQ Knowledge and CQ Action are the elements of CQ often given the most attention. Many short-term teams conduct extensive orientation, which includes researching some of the understanding necessary to make the trip meaningful. Many teams spend time talking about the importance of their behavior on the trip and remind one another about that during the trip. But little attention is given to the aspect of motivation when it comes to short-term missions or, for that matter, how it relates to cross-cultural interactions in general. The motivational component of cross-cultural adaptation is generally neglected or given little serious attention.[1]

Ironically, CQ Drive is the most important aspect when selecting people for cross-cultural work, including short-term missions work. As we saw in chapter 3, the way one anticipates and is motivated to participate in a short-term project directly influences how that individual experiences the trip. Motivation shapes cross-cultural engagement more than anything else. A person's primary motivation, whether to travel with friends or to "save" people, directly shapes how that person will engage with those he or she encounters.

It's not enough simply to be motivated to do short-term missions. Quite honestly, we're not short on passion and zeal when it comes to short-term missions. Many of our short-term endeavors are driven by our confidence that they're biblical, our love for adventure, or our desire to make a difference in the world. All these motivators powerfully shape our assumptions about what should happen on the trip. The question lies in whether we also see the importance of immersing ourselves in the local culture and how doing so will help us learn and serve.

CQ Drive doesn't happen in a vacuum. Our levels of motivation are connected to the motivations of those with whom we travel and, most of all, of those closest to us. Throughout the past couple of decades, as North Americans have traveled and worked abroad, a great deal of research has examined the role of one's family and friends in how an individual works cross-culturally. If you're really excited about going on an overseas assignment but your spouse or kids aren't, that has a direct impact on your level of motivation. If a close friend is on a trip with you and has little interest in really experiencing the culture, that immediately challenges your level of interest in engaging with the culture.

Motivation is also shaped by our cultural backgrounds. While we can't assume everyone from one place is more motivated than everyone from another place, it's important to understand the relationship between our cultural programming and how we're likely to score on CQ Drive. For example, Americans typically have lower success rates adjusting to other cultures compared to many other ethnic groups. There are a number of reasons for this. One of the primary contributing factors for our poor adaptation cross-culturally comes from the urgency factor we looked at earlier. We're programmed to solve problems and fix things efficiently. The very idea that we might go primarily to learn and relate goes against the grain of our cultural ethos. Furthermore, despite our espoused desire to learn from others, it's been ingrained in us as Americans that we're the best country in the world and we should therefore help other people become more like us. With that mind-set comes a whole set of assumptions that make it more challenging to calibrate our motivation for effective cross-cultural engagement.

In similar fashion, for many Americans, receiving positive feedback is a key motivator. I've often been a bit paralyzed in cross-cultural settings because I hear so little direct feedback on whether the ministry that's happening is effective. However, in many cultural contexts, directly expressing feedback—positive or negative—is viewed as a form of humiliation and embarrassment, so more discreet feedback is preferable. All of these cultural dynamics play a part in understanding CQ Drive.

In contrast, cultures that are more collectivist in their orientation—an idea we'll explore more fully in the next chapter—are motivated differently than those that are more individualistic (e.g., most Western cultures). Collectivists are motivated most by what's good for their group, not for each individual. For example, McDonald's wasn't successful in using its "Employee of the Month" program in India in the same way it uses it in North America. It was humiliating for most Indian employees to be singled out as the employee of the month. So McDonald's began rotating the award among teams of employees rather than singling out an individual.

One of the most important aspects of CQ Drive is our desire to adapt not only to the immediate task at hand but also to the culture as a whole. Typically, people who travel overseas to work, whether for business or for missions, are motivated to do their work well. An American businesswoman wants to run the branch office in Bangkok successfully. The Chicago pastor training in Ghana wants to feel as if he's communicated the content well with the people being trained. However, the same individuals often demonstrate a much lower level of motivation for adjusting to the culture as a whole. The US businesswoman in Thailand might think a ride down the Chau Phraya River in a river taxi has little to do with how she runs the office, and the North American pastor might think eating Ghanaian food has little influence on his teaching. The research demonstrates exactly the opposite. Our level of interest in connecting with a culture as a whole directly shapes how well we do our work in subtle but profound ways.

The same dynamics apply to short-term missions. Most short-term participants have low CQ Drive when it comes to truly engaging in the life of a culture. We have a strong desire to complete the roof project and do it well. We want to reach as many kids as possible through the vacation Bible school program we're running, or we want to really help the pastors we're training. Those are noble and worthy forms of motivation, but by themselves, they aren't enough. In fact, too much motivation to do our tasks well may impede our ability to engage with people. We're inclined to be so focused on our task that we miss out on some of the more important conversations and experiences. As a result, many of our short-term projects are done with a low level of CQ Drive. We end up observing the novelties of a new place from afar rather than really immersing ourselves in the context. We look for familiar foods and crave a current copy of *USA Today* on our way to paint the wall, and so we miss a huge part of the experience.

CQ Drive goes beyond simply the excitement of traveling to a new place. It's the perseverance required when the novelty wears off and the differences start to chafe at us. Given its importance and our tendency to neglect motivation, it's essential we consider a few ways to nurture CQ Drive.

Nurturing CQ Drive

Nurturing the desire and motivation to adapt cross-culturally is especially challenging when it involves a project as brief as ten days to two weeks. When expatriates move overseas for several years, they often have a much higher level of motivation to adapt because they're going to be there much longer and adapting to the local culture is essential for them to succeed. However, there's often little interest in working hard to adapt to a culture when you're only there for a few days. There are a number of ways to address this. Here are a few considerations.

Be Honest

A great deal of the research we've looked at in this book raises questions about the long-term impact of short-term missions. There is evidence that short-term missions can have a positive impact on both goers and receivers, but we need to look honestly at the questions raised by some of the findings. One of the things that continued to emerge when comparing the perspectives of North American short-termers and those of majority world church members was our exaggerated descriptions of what happens as a result of these trips.

Our motivation for short-term missions often involves an overstated description of what happens in others and us. We talk about changing entire communities that don't look all that different after we leave. We describe the lifelong changes in us, including our commitments to pray more and give more, but within six to eight weeks, most of us are praying and giving about the same as before the trip.[2]

There are compelling, redemptive reasons to engage in short-term missions. But in our need to defend our trips to ourselves and our supporters, we must not overstate the influence of the trips—upon us or those we serve. I have little trouble believing that some kind of transformation occurs when we leave the comforts of home to live in an entirely different part of the world for a couple weeks. Likewise, when a group of Mexicans hosts a group of North Americans for a week, surely there is some sort of impact. Every encounter in life plays at least some role in who I am and how I view the world and God. However, we need to move toward seeing our short-term missions trips as one of many life experiences that make an impact on us and others.

When we become more honest about seeing short-term missions trips as one of thousands of life experiences that change us, we'll be motivated more appropriately, which in turn will help us engage more effectively. Let's stop thinking about short-term missions as a service to perform and see it instead as another expression of living in the way of Jesus, which includes giving and receiving from our brothers and sisters in Christ globally. Let's think about missions as a time when we're responsible to learn. When we're with brothers and sisters from another part of the world, let's spend less time thinking about how we can tell everyone back home what we did for them and more time finding out what they're truly facing and getting their perspective on how we can help them and they can help us. Before we spend time painting a wall, let's spend time deciding if that's the best thing we can do. With high levels of unemployment in most of the places we visit, are we taking jobs away from people who need them when we do our building projects? There are probably times when it's appropriate to do a building project, but be willing to slow down and ask the question before jumping in.

This is challenging because often the request to build a building or to provide training comes from the local believers themselves. I encounter this all the time. I frequently interact with majority world church leaders who request curriculum and resources developed in the West. I don't doubt they can make use of them, but part of my being honest about their true needs means sometimes challenging even the requests that come from our majority world church brothers and sisters. The honesty we're after has to come from a broad perspective of what God is doing among people all over the world and continually learning what our role is in that. Sometimes we need to sacrifice our egos and say, "I'm not going to train. I want to do whatever I can to help you train your people using the material that's developed by your context for your context." Or we may need to say, "We're not going to build that. We're going to raise the money for you to employ your people to build it." Or maybe we refer them to another ministry that's already working effectively in their context who can better meet their needs.

As we pursue this kind of honest reflection, we begin to move away from the drive-by mission trip mentality. An accurate perspective on what can happen within others and us is the kind of honesty our supporters deserve, not to mention our brothers and sisters in Christ in the majority world and the others who live there. This kind of honesty is an essential part of nurturing CQ Drive. Over the long haul, we'll stay motivated far longer and persevere through much more cultural dissonance when we are honest about what we have to offer and what we have to gain.

Look for Relevance

Few of us are motivated to do something if it feels irrelevant and disconnected from our lives. In order to be motivated to persevere through the challenges of cross-cultural work, we must see how they relate to our other goals. This is a basic rule of learning. We aren't motivated to learn about things that we perceive to be irrelevant to our needs. The mind-set is, "If I have to learn algebra, help me see why I'll ever need it!" We have to see how eating unfamiliar foods, sitting through services in a foreign language, and touring ancient temples are relevant to God's call on our lives. It's imperative that we frame our experiences as pertinent and related to the overall goals of our lives.

The average short-term team won't see how eating at McDonald's every day could hinder their vacation Bible school program. Yet we need to see the subtle but profound connections between where we eat, where we stay, and how we interact with how we fulfill our mission tasks. We need to soak in the culture and set the tone for others traveling with us about the importance of cultural immersion for effective relationships and ministry. We need to persevere through difficult interactions, try the foods and the language, and seek to understand what's really going on beneath the surface of what we see. If you're leading a short-term missions trip, challenge your group members to experience as much of the culture as possible. Help them see how taking it all in can directly relate to fulfilling your mission—both your short-term mission and your lifelong calling to extend the redemptive mission of God.

Connect to CQ Knowledge

Finally, one of the best ways to improve CQ Drive is through the next CQ capability: CQ Knowledge. By learning about a culture, its history, and its values, we become more motivated to engage with it, particularly if we can see the relevance of cultural understanding to the mission at hand. And learning about a culture can help us persevere through the things that can otherwise be disorienting and stressful.

For example, a highly relational, empathetic North American who takes a short-term trip to a society that sees a big distinction between leaders and followers (something we'll later describe as "power distance") needs to relate and serve in light of what he knows about how the culture views status. Perhaps the North American thinks, *Forget about all these distinctions based on the color of skin or money. I'm going to show these people I don't believe in that*. Imagine he meets a low-status cleaning lady, stops to talk with her, and then gives her a warm embrace as he walks away. His desire to love her just as she is is commendable. However, she may miss entirely what he's trying to communicate because he violated the cultural norm about roles and status. This may well be an area in which visiting Christians need to be countercultural. However, the short-term missionary needs to understand that the cleaning lady may get a different message than he intended.

The first step in dealing with this is motivation. But once we are motivated to best demonstrate our love for God and people, we inevitably come to see the importance of understanding how to best communicate that love in the various cultures we encounter. Sheer willpower to effectively express love cross-culturally isn't enough, and neither is pure head knowledge about what a culture values. But together, CQ Drive and CQ Knowledge can play a powerful role in helping us effectively love and serve across borders. High CQ Drive helps us use our cross-cultural understanding to love God and love others.

Back to Shanghai

Brian had a great night of sleep, and he was ready to conquer a new day—even though he still wouldn't get to teach for a couple more days. Jun walked in the room, and everybody was sipping instant tea and coffee. "Breakfast has arrived," he said, as he set noodles and congee on the table.

Jun looked at a couple of the students and said, "You live close to Chicago—right?"

"Yeah, not too far," one of them replied.

"Shanghai looks pretty much like an American city, don't you think?" he asked.

A few of the students nervously chuckled.

After a few more minutes of small talk, Brian asked Jun for some more information about the teaching later that week. "How long will our sessions be? Can we freely share our faith? What do they know about our visit?" Jun didn't really answer his questions and just said things like, "Oh, they will really like you. This will be a very good week."

Seeing that he was getting nowhere, Brian thought he'd spend a few minutes looking over his teaching notes while he felt fresh. He said, "I'm going to grab a hazelnut latte! Anyone else want to join me at Starbucks around the corner?"

Jun said, "Oh, I'm so sorry. I don't know if we have time right now, Brian. Some of the university students have invited you to join them at Yuyuan Garden. Yuyuan Garden is said to be part of the Ming Dynasty. It's a peaceful, beautiful place right in the heart of the city, and a group of my students asked if you'll be their guests there for a while."

Brian asked, "Can I ask what 'a while' means?"

Jun said, "Don't worry. We'll just go for a while and see how you like it."

"Wow, that sounds really great," Brian continued. "My only concern is that I really need to spend some time preparing for class." Inside, Brian was thinking, *I don't need to hang out in some ancient garden! I'm not here to be a tourist. I want to be on top of my game to teach here.*

You see what's happening here. Brian is the epitome of the conscientious short-termer who wants to perform his task with excellence. He's to be affirmed for that. He knows teaching Chinese students isn't something that can be done just by winging it.

Unfortunately, Brian doesn't understand that one of the things that might help him most in teaching is spending time with a group of Chinese peers in a place they've invited him to come. A trip to the garden probably won't directly translate into teaching material; however, persevering through cultural experiences like this and, most of all, spending time with local students will be far more important to how he engages with his own students than he can imagine. Eating local food, walking down Nanjing Road, and lingering in Yuyuan Garden are probably what Brian needs far more to enhance his cultural intelligence and his effectiveness in teaching than spending a couple more hours reviewing his notes.

Strategies to Improve Your CQ Drive

Anytime:

1. Consider what cultures are most difficult for you. Why?
2. Connect cross-cultural engagement with your existing interests (e.g., art lovers can look at the way a culture views art;

sports enthusiasts can see how culture shapes the way people compete).

3. Get hands-on experiences with different cultures whenever you can.

On Your Short-Term Trip:

1. Notice your biases. How are you tempted to judge certain behaviors?
2. Create time to recharge your batteries—emotionally, spiritually, and physically.
3. Look for issues of injustice. Cultural intelligence is needed to make a difference. Seeing an injustice may increase your desire to serve with CQ.

10

Seek to Understand

CQ *Knowledge*

The team's first full day in Shanghai was devoted to following Jun and a few of his students around Shanghai. The tour included some of the typical spots for visitors such as the Yuyuan Garden, the Jade Buddha Temple, the Jin Mao Tower, and the Bund. They also went to some less touristy places such as a primary school, a market, and a neighborhood on the outer limits of the city.

By lunchtime, everyone was starving. Jun brought the team to one of his favorite restaurants. He smiled and said, "Well, I hope you're okay with the food here. I can't say it's the very best at this restaurant, but hopefully, it will be okay."

Jake blurted out, "Hey. We'll make the best of it. It's all part of the adventure!" Jun's smile seemed to fade slightly.

Jenny, one of the other team members, was trying to unpack what she thought Jun was trying to communicate. She had just taken a course in intercultural communication, and she felt something may be going on here that deserved attention. She began to wonder, *Is criticizing the food just a typical Chinese custom—something everyone does that really has nothing to do with the food itself? Or maybe he was trying to make a joke.* She remembered that humor is one of the hardest things to translate cross-culturally. Jun did have a big smile as he said it, so maybe he was trying to be funny. On the other hand, in the brief synopsis she had read about Chinese culture, she knew they made a practice of self-effacing. So perhaps that's what this was. Or was it the indirect approach often used by Chinese people when they interact? Or maybe this was Jun's backhanded way of expressing concern about whether the next three weeks of working together was a good idea.[1]

Just then Jenny realized Jun was talking to her. "What are you studying?" he asked her.

She replied, "Oh—I'm majoring in communications and I might minor in TESL." Then she said, "I heard you just graduated with an English major, Jun. What are you going to do next?"

"Oh. I already have a job at the university," he said.

"Congratulations. Have you found a place to live?" she asked.

"Actually, the university is right by my house," Jun replied.

"You mean your parents' house?" asked Jenny.

"Yes. Exactly. Our house," replied Jun.

"So are you going to save up some money for a while before you move out?" chimed in Jake.

Jun replied, "No. We're quite happy with our place."

Jake said, "Well, I guess that's not all bad until you're married anyway."

Jun said, "I am married."

Sarah, the only student on the team majoring in intercultural studies, said, "Oh yeah. All Asians do that." A couple of the other students rolled their eyes, both because they had been listening to Sarah's expertise on Asian culture every few minutes for the last couple days and because they couldn't imagine the thought of living with their parents after being married.

Jenny's mind began to wander again. *Why do so many generations here live together? That can't be healthy for marriage, can it? Or maybe we're the ones who aren't healthy by thinking we have to get out on our own.*

"Jenny!" Jake interrupted her thoughts. "The rice, please. Can you please pass the rice?"

At the surface level, Jenny's concerns are connected to her limited understanding of Chinese customs. Compared to Jake, who doesn't even notice that some miscommunication may be occurring, Jenny is aware that something isn't quite right, but she lacks the cultural intelligence to know what it is and how best to respond. How do we explain Sarah? We haven't heard much from her, but it appears the rest of the team has. Is she demonstrating the greatest measure of CQ Knowledge because she's devoted almost all her study to intercultural issues? We'll come back to these students in Shanghai in a bit. For now, let's look at the second capability of cultural intelligence: CQ Knowledge.

In recent years, a great deal of attention has been given to the importance of training people who participate in short-term missions. Leaders spend time preparing groups for what they should expect when they travel to their destination. Others invest time researching the history of the place, the people's views on religion, their language, and more. This, in part, is what growing in CQ Knowledge means.

What Is CQ Knowledge?

CQ Knowledge refers to our understanding about cross-cultural issues and differences. While this understanding includes the kinds of things done in many short-term orientation meetings, it's also more than just learning about the history and details of a particular culture. The most important part of CQ Knowledge is gaining a general understanding about how cultures vary. How does culture affect the way people view the world? How does that relate to the specific culture we're about to visit? How does it explain our own behavior? What's behind the common gestures used? These are the type of questions a person with high CQ Knowledge asks and understands. Growing in CQ Knowledge requires more than simply reading the *Lonely Planet Guide* for the country we're about to visit; it involves an ongoing process of looking at cultures and beginning to understand how they vary.

Cultural understanding begins with understanding what culture is in the first place. Anthropologists and sociologists have argued for years about how to define culture, but most agree that culture is the collective beliefs people hold about how things should be and how one should behave. It's a way of looking at the values, attitudes, and beliefs shared by a common group of people. While things such as food, art, and literature give us visible expressions of culture, one of the greatest challenges that comes with understanding culture is that cultural knowledge is largely invisible. So when we talk about serving with eyes wide open, the vision we're trying to enhance is the ability to see what isn't immediately visible to the physical eye. It's looking beyond the driving habits, diet, and architecture to see what lies beneath those things. That's what CQ Knowledge allows us to do.

Think of culture as the software that runs our minds. It's the mental programming that shapes our habits, beliefs, decision making, and the way we see the world.[2] This programming is passed along from generation to generation. Cultural programming applies to national and ethnic groups, to organizations (such as the culture of a particular company or church), and even to subcultural groups such as adolescents, political parties, or evangelicals. While CQ Knowledge can enhance interactions in any of these cultural groups, our interest is primarily in national culture—the socioethnic cultures of people living in the communities we're visiting on our short-term trips.

An easy way to see how culture programs our minds is to look at the views people from different cultures have of dogs. My daughter Emily loves dogs. She always has. She stops to pet every one of them and volunteers at our local vet's. If she had her way, our home would be filled with dogs. Emily, like many Westerners, sees dogs not as mere animals but as members of the family. Even those of us who aren't dog lovers think of dogs as belonging in people's homes and yards, not as animals that should be left to roam wild on their own. In North America, dogs eat with us, watch TV with us, and go on vacation with us. It's becoming more and more common in suburbs around the US to find boutiques devoted exclusively to dogs. In contrast, many people living in Islamic cultures view dogs as animals to be avoided at all costs. They see dogs like the typical North American sees rats or pigs. In their minds, dogs are dirty animals that are primarily a nuisance. In still other parts of the world, dogs are considered an exotic delicacy, served to the most honored guests.

Which is the "right" view of dogs? This is the kind of instance when we can be tempted to misuse the Bible. North American dog lovers might find a verse that proves their view of dogs. Certainly, there are values (and verses) that direct how we should treat all animals, including dogs. But we're hard-pressed to make a biblical case for or against any of these cultural differences in how people view dogs. That may seem wrong to you, because our view of dogs is so ingrained in us through the mental programming of our culture.

CQ Knowledge helps us move beyond seeing the stray dogs roaming throughout Indonesia as simply neglected pets to consider how Indonesians' interactions with dogs reflect their cultural values and assumptions. Applying CQ Knowledge becomes more challenging when dealing with issues such as how a culture views polygamy or literacy or the Bible, but it's even more important with these weightier issues.

CQ Knowledge is essential because it's at the core of serving with eyes wide open. CQ Knowledge gives us a healthy starting point for more effectively engaging in short-term missions. Many of the pitfalls of short-term missions could be avoided with CQ Knowledge. But the point is not to master CQ Knowledge before we take off on our next trip. We continue to grow in CQ Knowledge throughout our lifetime. Here are a few ways to begin improving our CQ Knowledge.

Nurturing CQ Knowledge

If we're going to Mexico, reading about some basic habits of Mexican people is a good starting point. In order to truly nurture our CQ Knowledge, however, we need to go beyond that. We need to look at a broader perspective of cultural understanding by exploring some key categories of cross-cultural difference. CQ Knowledge is mostly about understanding some primary ways cultures differ according to what people in those cultures value. We have to beware of carelessly applying these values to everyone from a culture, but understanding these values is a helpful way to begin. To nurture our CQ Knowledge, we need to look at five dimensions that are commonly used to understand and measure cultural differences: time, context, individualism, power distance, and uncertainty avoidance. Many more than these exist, but these are some of the most important ones for nurturing CQ Knowledge, particularly for short-term missions trips.

Event Time versus Clock Time

Most of us are pretty familiar with the way people from different cultures view time. We can easily think of cultures in which people are routinely punctual and those in which people are chronically "late." We can't stereotype people too quickly, but this kind of understanding is precisely what we're after in developing CQ Knowledge.

In his book *A Geography of Time*, Robert Levine explores the role of industrialization in how a culture views time.[3] According to Levine, industrialization promotes an ethos of producing and consuming. As a result, people in those cultures live by "clock time." Punctuality and efficiency rule the day. A great deal of what we considered as part of the urgency issue in part 2 is an expression of our clock-time orientation. The clock is what determines when things start and end. Respect, excellence, and conscientiousness are communicated by our punctuality.

In contrast, less-industrialized cultures are far more interested in the priority and obligation of social relationships. Levine refers to these cultures as "event-time" cultures. Events begin and end when all the participants feel the time is right rather than what the clock says. Spontaneity is a core value among these people. A South American talked about the birthday party he threw for his son while they were living in the United States. They invited friends from the US and friends from Latin America. The invitation said the party would be from 2:00 to 4:00 p.m. on Saturday. The friends from the US showed up at 2:00 and left around 4:00. In contrast, several of the Latinos came thirty to ninety minutes late and stayed well past 4:00 p.m. Some of them remained until 2:00 the next morning. One Argentinean friend asked the father why the invitation listed an ending time. He was offended by the implication that there was a time limit on how long they could be together.[4]

What's the time orientation of people in the culture you're visiting on your short-term trip? Understanding alone can't prepare you for all the challenges that may come with opposing views of time, but it's a good start. If you're going with a team of people, spend some time anticipating how your approach to time may frustrate the locals who host you. How may their time orientation frustrate you? And what can you learn from each other's view of time?

High Context versus Low Context

Another important category used to describe cultural differences is high context versus low context. High context refers to places where people have a lot of history together. Things operate in high-context cultures as if everyone there is an insider and knows how to behave. Written instructions and explicit directions are minimal because most people know what to do and how to think.

Our families are probably the most tangible examples of high-context environments. After years of being together, we know what the unspoken rules are of what we eat, how we celebrate holidays, and how we communicate with each other. Many of our church cultures are the same. We know when to sit, stand, and participate. Some national cultures are high-context too. In places such as Latin America, Korea, and the Middle East, information is much more likely to be assumed and embedded within people rather than explicitly stated. There aren't a lot of signs or detailed information about how to act. High-context cultures can be difficult places to visit as an outsider.

Places such as Western Europe and the United States are low-context cultures. Many of our connections with people and places are of a shorter duration; therefore, less is assumed. Instructions about where to park, how to flush the toilet, and where to order food are often displayed. Low-context cultures can be easier to enter than high-context cultures, because even if you're an outsider, much of the information needed to participate is explicit. Extra attention is given to providing information about how to act.[5]

Spend some time thinking about how your short-term trip will be affected by whether you're headed to a high-context or a low-context environment. As North Americans, we're often frustrated by life in a high-context environment. Signs at the airport may seem unclear, and locals may spend little time giving us instructions about how to order in a restaurant. But as we begin to see the realities of high and low contexts, we begin to grow in CQ Knowledge.

Individualism versus Collectivism

The next three areas come from the work of Geert Hofstede, one of the most important intercultural researchers. The first cultural value Hofstede researched is individualism versus collectivism.[6] This refers to one's primary source of identity.

One day some friends in Singapore were explaining to me how Singaporean students are put in career tracks as early as fourth or fifth grade. Teachers assess students' areas of strength, such as writing or math, and begin to groom them for vocations that match those strengths. As a result, by the time Singaporean students get ready to graduate from high school, it's pretty clear what path they're going to take—whether medicine, teaching, or technology. However, the universities and technical institutes have a limited number of openings for each area, so after the quotas are reached for premed students or education students, for example, young people are directed into other career paths.

As I listened to this, I aborted any sense of cultural intelligence and said, "That's so unfair! Why can't the Singaporean system empower people to pursue their dreams instead of prescribing everyone's future?"

They listened to me continue my rant then calmly responded, "You're assuming we place as much importance on personal dreams and goals as North Americans do. For us, the individual is not what's most important. Our collective society is what we value. If we have an overabundance of physicians and a shortage of teachers, we won't be sustained as a society. If there aren't enough people in the technical workforce, we'll be overrun by other, much larger countries."

I'm not ready to abandon encouraging people to pursue their personal callings, but this conversation exposed me to my individualist orientation versus their collectivist orientation.

The United States scores higher than any other national culture on Hofstede's scale of individualism. And Singapore and China are the most collectivist cultures examined by Hofstede. Cultures that score high on the individualism scale are places where people are most concerned about the life, rights, and concerns of the individual. Decisions are based on what an individual deems is best for his or her life. Nowhere is this more apparent than in our own culture. Nowadays, the American dream seems less characterized by having a four-bedroom house with a white picket fence, a minivan, and 2.5 kids than by being able to say, "I'll think what I want, do what I want, go where I want, and be responsible to no one but myself."

In contrast, people in collectivist cultures view themselves less autonomously and more as members of groups. They're concerned about the effects of actions on the group as a whole, and decisions are made by consensus rather than individually. This isn't to say people living in collectivist cultures are naturally unselfish. Rather, they're programmed to think first about the goals and needs of the groups of which they're a part rather than their own individual needs.

Neither end of the continuum is a complete picture of how God calls us to live. Our focus on the individual coincides with the personal attention and responsibility God gives us. Jesus seems very interested in individuals as well as entire families and nations. He calls people to personally follow him. At the same time, our obsession with personal interests and our quest for individual spiritual growth are not a complete reflection of how we're to live. Scripture is full of examples in which God speaks to communities rather than to individuals. For example, almost every reference to "spiritual maturity" in the New Testament is to a plural audience. I'm not called to resist sin or pursue God by myself, and the goal of my spiritual maturity isn't just for me. I'm called to mature *with* my brothers and sisters in the faith, *for* the sake of my brothers and sisters in the faith—both my local church community and the community of God's people all over the world past, present, and future.

As we begin to open our eyes to the varying ways cultures view the individual, we see an important area that affects our CQ Knowledge. The college students listening to Jun talk about living with his parents considered first and foremost what Jun would want for himself rather than what might be best for his entire family. Furthermore, Jun didn't seem to pick up that the students found his living situation unusual. A greater measure of understanding about the varying beliefs cultures have about individuals and groups such as families could increase the cultural intelligence of the North American students and Jun.

Power Distance

Power distance refers to the social distance between leaders and followers. Countries that score high in power distance—such as Mexico, India, and Ghana—offer a great deal of formal respect to leaders. Titles and status are revered, leaders and followers are unlikely to socialize together, and subordinates are not expected to question their superiors. High power distance cultures are usually also very collectivist.

Linda and I have had African friends in our home who are amazed at the amount of voice we give our girls in everyday decisions. It's second nature for us to give them a choice of what they want for breakfast, the interests they want to pursue, and even where we should go on vacation together. And when they aren't sure they fully agree with something we espouse, we encourage them to ask the "why" question. We expect them to question respectfully, but the asking itself is welcome. This reflects the individualism and low power distance that exist in our parenting style. We're trying to prepare our girls to make decisions on their own, and we want them to have a voice in our family decisions—clearly a very North American approach to family life. North Americans score much lower on the power distance scale than most Africans do.

International students from high power distance cultures who come to study in the United States often demonstrate discomfort with our attitudes toward authority figures. A student from Iran said, "The first time my professor told me, 'I don't know the answer—I will have to look it up,' I was shocked. I asked myself, 'Why is he teaching me?' In my country a professor would give a wrong answer rather than admit ignorance."[7]

A student from Indonesia, a culture that scores even higher than Iran in power distance, made this comment: "I was surprised and confused when on leaving Whittier Hall the provost, in person, held the door for me in order to let me pass before he would enter the door. I was so confused that I could not find the words to express my gratefulness, and I almost fell on my knees as I would certainly do back home. A man who is by far my superior is holding the door for me, a mere student and a nobody."[8]

The United States by no means scores lowest on the scale of power distance. Canada, Germany, and Finland score lower. And Austria and Israel are among the lowest power distance cultures in the world. In these contexts, followers feel at ease socializing with their leaders and addressing them as peers. Students feel free to question their pastors, teachers, and parents, and they expect to have input in the decision-making process.

I have antibodies in my system for dictatorial, top-down, hierarchical styles of leadership. I'm much more comfortable with an egalitarian approach in which teams create vision with the input of many voices. However, I must be careful not to biblicize my cultural preferences regarding power distance. Altough the Bible has much to say about the importance of serving and sharing leadership, we have to avoid proof-texting team-based approaches to leadership that are really more culturally based than biblically based. After all, there are far more biblical examples of hierarchical leadership than team-based leadership. But those from high power distance cultures must also be careful not to presume that their cultural preferences are the only biblical way to lead. Are the hierarchical examples of leadership in the Bible an outgrowth of the cultures in which they took place, or are they directives intended by God?

Considering the relationship between so-called high-status people and low-status people and between leaders and followers is an important area in which we must continue to grow in understanding. The short-term participants who engage in cultural intelligence will avoid writing off an offensive leadership style they encounter cross-culturally and instead will seek to understand it.

Uncertainty Avoidance

Finally, uncertainty avoidance is the extent to which a culture is at ease with risk and unpredictability. Cultures that score high in uncertainty avoidance are places where people have been programmed to have little tolerance for the unknown. They focus on ways to reduce uncertainty and ambiguity, and they create structures to help ensure some measure of predictability. For example, cultures such as Greece, Japan, and France want clear instructions and predictable timetables for completing assignments in order to reduce any ambiguity.

On the other hand, cultures low in uncertainty avoidance, such as Britain, Jamaica, and Sweden, are not as threatened by unknown situations and what lies ahead. Open-ended instructions, varying ways of doing things, and loose deadlines are more typical in countries with low scores in uncertainty avoidance.

There is a high correlation between this cultural dimension and the way a culture approaches time. Clock-time cultures tend to be higher on the uncertainty avoidance scale than event-time cultures. Understanding this particular dimension is also a way to understand the differences that exist between two cultures that may otherwise seem to be much the same. For example, Germany and Great Britain have a great deal in common. Both are in Western Europe, both speak a Germanic language, both had relatively similar populations before the German reunification, and the British royal family is of German descent. But the person who understands the uncertainty avoidance dimension will quickly notice considerable differences between life in Frankfurt and life in London. Punctuality, structure, and order are modus operandi in German culture, whereas Brits are much more easygoing and less concerned about precision. This can be explained in part due to the different views the cultures have toward the unknown.

Keep in mind that these are generalizations. For example, while Australians are listed as having a clock-time orientation, someone observing the South Sea Islanders in Australia would find that laughable. The South Sea Islanders are very much oriented by event time. Similar exceptions exist in each of the countries or regions listed. But these scores provide some sense of the differences we must understand to strengthen our CQ Knowledge.

Exploring the differences between how people view time, status, and uncertainty are the types of issues central to developing CQ Knowledge. One of the most effective ways to think through and understand the implications of these dynamics is to use case studies from different cultures that demonstrate how these differences play out. Books such as Robert L. Kohls and John M. Knight's *Developing Intercultural Awareness* and Craig Storti's *Cross-Cultural Dialogues* are some of the best resources available for such exercises.

In addition, interactive learning, conversations, and readings related to cultural differences are helpful in gaining understanding about cross-cultural differences. These, coupled with our cross-cultural experiences, provide a powerful way of nurturing CQ Knowledge. We'll look more specifically at the role of travel itself in nurturing both knowledge and CQ Strategy in the next chapter. For now, suffice it to say that international experiences coupled with good information about cross-cultural differences are the most effective means of nurturing CQ Knowledge.[9]

We'll have a better perspective on our short-term missions trips if we think about the values explored in this chapter. We need to understand both the general dimensions of cross-cultural differences and the ways

Estimates of Cultural Value Orientations[10]

Take a look at how these regions score in these five areas. These are estimates and serve as a first "best guess."

Global Clusters	Time Orientation	Context	Collectivist	Power Distance	Uncertainty Avoidance
Nordic Europe Denmark, Finland, Norway, Sweden, etc.	Clock	Low	Med	Low	Low
Anglo Australia, Canada, Ireland, New Zealand, South Africa (white), U.K., U.S., etc.	Clock	Low	Low	Low	Low
Germanic Europe Austria, Belgium, Germany, Netherlands, Switzerland, etc.	Clock	Low	Med	Low	Med
Eastern Europe Albania, Bulgaria, Czech Republic, Estonia, Greece, Hungary, Latvia, Lithuania, Poland, Romania, Russia, Serbia, Slovakia, Slovenia, etc.	Event*	High	Med*	Med	High
Latin Europe France, Italy, Portugal, Spain, etc.	Event	Med	Med	Med	High
Latin America Argentina, Bolivia, Brazil, Colombia, Costa Rica, Ecuador, El Salvador, Guatemala, Mexico, Venezuela, etc.	Event	Med	High*	High	High
Confucian Asia China (minus Japan and Singapore), Hong Kong, South Korea, Taiwan, etc.	Clock	High	High	Med	Low
Japan and Singapore	Clock	High	High	Med	High
Southern Asia India, Indonesia, Malaysia, Philippines, Thailand, etc.	Event*	High	High	High*	Med
Sub-Sahara Africa Namibia, Nigeria, South Africa (black), Zambia, Zimbabwe, etc.	Event	High	High	Med	Med
Arab Algeria, Bahrain, Egypt, Iraq, Jordan, Kuwait, Lebanon, Libya, Morocco, Oman, Qatar, Saudi Arabia, Syria, Tunisia, Turkey, UAE, Yemen, etc.	Event	High	High	High	Med

*Denotes countries within the region that may have wide variance in this particular value (e.g. some Eastern European cultures are quite individualistic and others are quite collectivist).

those dimensions play out in the specific cultures we're going to visit. In addition, the issues explored in part 2—motivation, urgency, common ground, the Bible, money, and simplicity—are the areas in which we need to grow in our understanding of how our cultural programming as North Americans affects the way we do short-term missions.

The danger in approaching CQ Knowledge through the categories described in this chapter is that we can repeat the very pitfalls we looked at earlier, wherein we oversimplify. We can too easily ignore personality differences that are as complex as cultural differences. My wife, Linda, thrives in event-time cultures. She loves to be spontaneous and cares little about watching the clock. I find event time a welcome change for a couple days of vacation, but then I'm ready to get back to structure, start-and-end times, and punctuality. We need to develop CQ Knowledge based on more than just one or two individuals. This is precisely why CQ Knowledge alone does not equal cultural intelligence. It's only one of four interdependent capabilities.

Back in Shanghai

How might CQ Knowledge shed light on what happened when Jun said, "I can't say the food is the very best at this restaurant, but hopefully it will be okay"?

What about Jun's comment about living with his parents? Sarah, the intercultural studies major, was the only one not surprised when Jun said he and his wife have no intentions of moving out. Is she the one who has CQ Knowledge here?

Meanwhile, Jenny, the reflective one on the team, has enough understanding of Chinese culture to sense Jun's apparent discomfort with the conversation. But she doesn't know how to make sense of it all.

As we move through the other CQ capabilities, we'll continue to use the students' short-term missions experience in Shanghai to shed light on how CQ intersects with short-term missions. For now, we can see a few different expressions of CQ Knowledge among Jake, Jenny, and Sarah. Jake's had more cross-cultural experience than anyone on the team, having grown up in Mexico. His experiential knowledge base of cross-cultural issues is pretty high. Does that make him a natural at responding to Jun? It gives him a head start in developing

CQ Knowledge, but without the other three areas, there's no guarantee Jake's experience will make him any more culturally intelligent than someone who has never left the United States. And he doesn't seem very knowledgeable about Chinese culture.

Jenny has a surface-level understanding of Chinese culture, but it does little to help her. She has some crude stereotypes about the way Chinese people tend to be indirect or self-effacing. However, she lacks the cultural intelligence to see how her individualist perspective shapes her view of Jun's living situation, and she isn't sure how to interpret the apology for the food at the restaurant.

If the students had a greater degree of CQ Knowledge, they would have known that it is customary in China to show respect for guests by disparaging one's own accomplishments, even the selection of a restaurant. In turn, the guest is expected to repay this respect with a compliment. When Jake simply said, "We'll make the best of it," he made a cultural blunder with Jun.[11]

Jake, Jenny, and Sarah's various forms of preparation to understand Chinese culture are a part of CQ, but by themselves they aren't enough. In some cases, CQ Knowledge by itself can be worse than no CQ Knowledge at all. Watch Sarah in the next couple chapters to see what that looks like!

Strategies to Improve Your CQ Knowledge

Anytime:

1. Study yourself and your own cultures.
2. Read a novel or watch a movie that is set in a different culture.
3. Study the Scriptures through the eyes of someone from a different culture.

On Your Short-Term Trip:

1. Buy a copy of *USA Today* and a copy of a local newspaper. Compare stories.
2. Talk to taxi drivers and hear their perspectives on life in this place.
3. Go to a grocery store. Notice what's sold and how it's advertised.

11

On Second Thought

CQ Strategy

Jenny has taken a couple TESL courses along with her communications major. She thought TESL might be something she'd be interested in pursuing. In some ways, the last couple days touring Shanghai with Jun's students has increased her confidence to teach English. On the other hand, she feels less prepared. Visiting places like the Jade Buddha Temple or the local primary school made her realize that while the students she'll be teaching are basically her peers, they've grown up with an entirely different perspective on faith and education.

Jenny discussed this with Jake on a run together. Jake said, "Jen, you've got to lighten up! You're being too hard on yourself and too analytical. People are people. I mean, most of Jun's students seem pretty much like us. For that matter, they're a whole lot like my Mexican friends back home too. Look at that, for example," he said, pointing to the cinema where most of the new releases were the same things playing in theaters back home. "And look at that," he said, pointing to Starbucks, "and that," pointing across the street to KFC. "The world is more and more the same everywhere, and that's especially true for our generation. Don't look at these students as Chinese. Just see them as people like you and me!"

"I hear what you're saying," Jen said. "But we also just ran by a local restaurant serving cat for lunch, and every store has an altar in front. That's nothing like the world back home!"

"Sure," said Jake. "But you're overthinking it again. Just have fun with it today. Basically, we get to talk with people who drink strong coffee like we do, listen to Coldplay like we do, and enjoy a good sushi dinner like we do. God can overcome the differences that are there. He wants these people saved. So just be yourself."

"Yeah. You're right, I guess," Jen said, though not entirely convinced.

How does cultural intelligence shed light on these interactions? Jenny's questions and awareness reflect some of the ideas behind CQ Strategy. CQ Strategy helps us to take our motivation and knowledge and put them to use before, during, and after our short-term missions experiences.

What Is CQ Strategy?

CQ Strategy is the degree to which we're mindful and aware when we interact cross-culturally, and it's our ability to plan in light of that awareness. CQ Strategy helps us turn off the cruise control we typically use as we interact with people so that we can intentionally question our assumptions. As we interpret the cues received through CQ Strategy, we continually adjust our CQ Knowledge and plan for how to behave appropriately.

I learned how to drive on my brother's stick-shift car. I sat at the traffic light, fully focused on the timing of the gas, clutch, and shift. I remember looking at the drivers in the cars around me who seemed to be doing anything *but* focusing on what they were doing. It looked as if driving was second nature to them, as if their cars were on continuous cruise control.

Now that I've been driving for more than twenty-five years, I jump in my car and drive without thinking. I drive miles at a time without giving a second thought to what I'm doing. Sometimes I'll be driving down the highway and suddenly realize I don't have a clue where I am. It's not that I'm being reckless; my mind just goes into cruise control as I drive along the open road.

When I drive in new places, and especially when I drive in cultures where the rules are different, I'm much more alert. Driving on the left side of the road takes a much higher degree of mental awareness on my part. I have to suspend the mental cruise control and give all my attention to my driving.

When we're in our own culture, we move in and out of many kinds of interactions and events on mental cruise control. We don't have to work extra hard to understand what someone means by a cliché they throw out or the embrace they offer before we walk away. When we interact cross-culturally, all that changes, or at least it should. We need to suspend mental cruise control and pay close attention to the cues. The process of becoming more aware is what CQ Strategy is about.

CQ Strategy is the ability to connect our knowledge with what we're observing in the real world. It's developing the awareness to see and interpret cues from our cross-cultural encounters. It's about making connections between what we know and what we're seeing and experiencing. It allows us to question our assumptions as well as the assumptions of others. As we grow in CQ Strategy, we begin using cross-cultural interactions as a way to reframe how we think about particular people, circumstances, or even the world as a whole.

Let me explain CQ Strategy this way. Soon Ang, one of the pioneering researchers of CQ, is a dear friend and colleague who lives and works in Singapore. Shortly after Soon and I first met in the US, we agreed to meet together again during my upcoming visit to Singapore.

Soon suggested we meet at Empires Café in the Raffles Hotel in Singapore. Raffles Hotel is in a part of town familiar to most visitors and just a block away from one of the major metro train stops. The menu at Empires Café is neatly divided between Western and Asian entrées. Knowing that I come from a low-context culture, Soon explained the menu to me and made sure I understood the Asian entrées in case I was interested. She pointed out a couple entrées in both the Western and the Asian section that she considered excellent.

We simultaneously viewed the menu and engaged in some small talk for a few minutes. Soon asked how many times I had been to Singapore. I told her I've been visiting Singapore for several years, including having lived there for a while with my family.

"How do you find the local food?" she asked.

When I listed *laksa* and *char kway teow* as some of my favorites, she began to interact with me a bit differently.

Soon's initial perception of me was limited to my being a North American ministry leader involved in graduate-level education and someone interested in applying CQ to mission work. Her CQ Knowledge gave her some understanding of what that might mean for me. The longer she talked with me, however, the more she reframed her interactions to line up with her new assumptions about me and my familiarity with Singapore.

Soon told me she purposely chose Empires Café because she knew it would be easy to find, and she wasn't sure of my level of comfort with Asian food. Likewise, she wasn't sure I would want to eat just Western food, so she chose a place with both options. As we began talking, I sent her cues that demonstrated my ease with Singaporean culture. She spent less time explaining the educational system and cultural dynamics because she adjusted her assumptions about me based on the cues she received from our interaction. Her awareness in the moment combined with her CQ Knowledge allowed her to develop a strategy or plan for how to interact with me effectively.

At one level, you could simply call Soon's behavior "empathetic listening," but it's more than that. Soon considered the possible cultural dynamics at work for both of us and then adjusted her assumptions from that understanding in light of our unfolding interaction together. She exercised the interpretive dimension of CQ (or CQ Strategy) that she spends so much time researching in others.[1]

CQ Strategy would have helped the short-term participants described in part 2. The students who assumed smiles meant everyone in Ecuador is happy would have stopped to ask if that's what the smiles really meant. Trainers who interpreted attentive students' behavior as hunger for the material would have asked whether that's what they really were communicating nonverbally.

CQ Strategy follows a three-step process. First, CQ Strategy begins with *awareness*. Soon's understanding and experience with North Americans made her aware that meeting at a certain restaurant might be more comfortable for me. Then as we began to interact, she continued to pay attention to cues. Some people are naturally more observant than others, but all of us can grow in our ability to watch for cues—both explicit and implicit—sent by people and events we encounter cross-culturally. This is what Soon was doing as she listened to me describe my previous experiences in Singapore. Some of the cues I sent were subtle. I asked where she lives, and when she told me, I referenced a nearby landmark, which demonstrated to her my awareness of Singapore beyond what would be typical of the novice visitor. She became aware of my frame of reference by what I did and didn't say.

Second, CQ Strategy helps us *plan* our cross-cultural interactions. Soon planned both before we got together (where to meet and how to interact together about our work) and in the midst of our interaction. People going on short-term missions trips that involve teaching, preaching, or making any kind of presentation need to plan how to present the content specifically as it relates to the particular cultural context, as compared to how it would be taught at home. In addition, planning must include how to most appropriately interact with authority figures and members of the opposite sex, how to approach conflict situations, and so on. Awareness and planning are directly related to CQ Knowledge. Understanding a culture's score in individualism or power distance aids us in planning our encounter.

Checking and monitoring is the final step in CQ Strategy. This is when we compare what we planned with what's actually happening. If we change an assumption, we need to test that altered assumption with other encounters and experiences. When appropriate, we can even talk about what we're observing with the people we encounter in another context. We need to exercise caution here, however. Just as we need to question our own assumptions underlying our behavior, we can't assume that another's perspective about their behavior is based on accurate assumptions.

Those with high CQ Strategy possess an ongoing awareness of what's going on around them beyond what they can see with their physical eyes. They possess a mindfulness that makes them aware and thus able to more accurately interpret unfamiliar behaviors and events.

Nurturing CQ Strategy

While all four CQ capabilities can improve the way we do short-term missions, this is the area I want to nurture most through this book. Serving with eyes wide open goes against the grain of our fast-paced, urgent culture by helping us reflect on and question our assumptions. Reflection doesn't mean we should sit in isolation in a serene setting to write in our journals all day long. Instead, we have to learn to engage in reflection and interpretation even when we're dead tired in the midst of Shanghai's city center. This is another reason CQ Drive is important.

The challenge is not *whether* people can think reflectively and intellectually but *how* to foster it in them. Obviously, some individuals and cultures are more analytically inclined than others, but CQ Strategy can be nurtured and encouraged in all of us. There are a number of ways to nurture CQ Strategy, including:

- Be aware of your own assumptions, ideas, and emotions as you engage cross-culturally.
- Look for ways to discover the assumptions of others through their words and behavior.
- Use all your senses to read a situation rather than just hearing the words or seeing the nonverbals.
- View every situation from several different perspectives by using an open mind.
- Create new categories/paradigms for seeing things.
- Seek out fresh information to confirm or disconfirm new categories.
- Use empathy to try to identify.[2]

Stepping back to think reflectively and question our assumptions is one of the biggest needs in short-term missions work. Suggestions like the ones above are a good start, but we need more guidance and help in nurturing this area that is so desperately lacking in much of our short-term work. Here are some ways to begin the process.

Stimulate Your Imagination

Stimulating our imaginative capacity is one of the most important ways to nurture CQ Strategy. Stories, narratives, myths, tales, and rituals capture aspects of the world in ways not readily available through more traditional, bullet-point approaches to understanding cross-cultural differences. The dimensions we considered in nurturing

CQ Knowledge—individuality, power distance, and event time versus clock time—are essential starting points for interacting effectively cross-culturally. However, reading fiction and biographies of people from various cultures will also help us see the more subtle assumptions and paradigms underlying cultural values. Stimulate your imagination by reading novels and biographies about and by people in the places you're going. Before going on your short-term missions trip, ask multiple people who live there about their favorite novels or movies. Use those to get into the mental programming of the culture.

Even if you make annual treks to the Czech Republic and want to focus all your cross-cultural understanding on the Czech context, spend some time reading pieces about and by people in other cultural contexts as well. Reading narrative pieces from a diversity of cultural perspectives will further enhance your ability to interpret cultural cues and recognize differences. Few things enhance CQ Strategy as does this kind of reading.

If this kind of literature is new to you, let me recommend a few books. Khaled Hosseini's novel *The Kite Runner* is one of the best books I've read. While you may not be taking a short-term trip to Afghanistan, the story written by this Afghan is sure to challenge your cultural assumptions in many areas. Or try reading Jhumpa Lahiri's *The Namesake: A Novel* to gain perspective on the different assumptions Indian couples, even Indian Americans, use in naming their children. I've made several references throughout this book to Richard Dooling's *White Man's Grave*. The language and witchcraft in Dooling's story are not for the lighthearted, but it's a compelling picture of life in West Africa. Of course, there's also much to be gained from the true stories of Brother Yun in *The Heavenly Man* or Nelson Mandela in *The Long Walk to Freedom*.

Reading novels and memoirs related to cross-cultural situations is one of the most powerful ways to nurture our minds to think creatively and reflectively. In addition, we can stimulate our imagination by simply forcing ourselves to do routine things differently. Taking an alternate route to work, ordering a different kind of coffee, and changing the order of our morning routine will impact our ability to think outside the normal paradigms of our lives.

As you can see, nurturing CQ Strategy has implications that far surpass the journey of our short-term missions trip. It's the opportunity to begin viewing the world around us in new and significant ways.

Open or Close Your Window

Another way to nurture CQ Strategy involves adjusting the way we interact with others. Successful communication depends on accurately reading the cues of those with whom we interact. Introverted people reveal little and tend to keep the windows into their lives closed as they interact with others. Others who are more extroverted reveal more of themselves and keep their windows open. Most of us tend to keep our window relatively small when we're in new and unfamiliar situations. In contrast, we tend to share more of ourselves when we're with familiar people and in places where we feel safe and comfortable. With certain individuals and in certain settings, even the gregarious and extroverted are wise to open less of themselves. In other situations, even the painfully introverted need to open up more as a way to interact appropriately. This communication skill is important anytime we interact with others, but it's especially important for cross-cultural conversations.

While personality differences exist throughout cultures, cultures as a whole have a style of relating and communicating that they deem most appropriate. The person with a growing measure of CQ Strategy learns how to read cues from both individuals and a culture at large. In knowing how much of ourselves to reveal, we are not trying to be a chameleon or to be whatever we think another person wants us to be. Instead, we are learning to interpret cues in order to adapt our communication and behavior in a way that puts the other person at ease. Envision yourself as a mirror to the people with whom you're speaking. What's the cadence of their speech? How loudly do they talk? What's their body language? By adjusting your behavior to mirror theirs, they'll automatically feel more comfortable. "This doesn't mean, of course, that you should be disingenuous. Rather, it shows that you're particularly sensitive to other people's emotional temperaments. You're just tweaking your style to ensure that the windows remain wide open."[3] Practice this in your next conversation.

Journal

One of the most valuable tools for nurturing CQ Strategy is journaling. Some people journal quite naturally, while others find it incredibly difficult. Much of my research on short-term missions has included both my own journaling and the journals of other short-termers who graciously allowed me to read their thoughts. Participants most often wrote about what they did each day, along with some prayer requests. That's a good start to journaling, but it's only the beginning of learning to journal as a way to nurture an ability to interpret cues in cross-cultural interactions.

Equally important in describing our observations is thinking about the meaning behind those observations and experiences. Writing allows us to understand our lives and others in ways that few other things do. It forces us to slow down and become aware of our surroundings. Journal writing enhances our ability to interpret the barrage of cues surrounding us during our short-term trips.

Commit to spending some time journaling on your next trip. Do it before you leave, while you're there, and after you come home. Do more than simply record the events of each day. Describe things that make you uncomfortable. Write down questions that come to mind. What insights are you gaining? What are you seeing about yourself, others, and God? How might your faith be different if you had grown up in this culture instead of at home? Read your journal out loud to someone you trust. Journaling like this can be a vital source of cultural intelligence for you.

Immerse Yourself Cross-Culturally

At the risk of missing the obvious, few things have the ability to nurture CQ Strategy like actual cross-cultural experiences. As we've seen countless times in this journey, experience alone doesn't ensure growth in our ability to interpret what's occurring cross-culturally. In fact, if we fail to engage with a reflective spirit whereby we question the assumptions of ourselves and others, immersing ourselves cross-culturally can actually be a detriment to improving CQ. We can end up perpetuating erroneous assumptions and stereotypes in others and ourselves by failing to engage in CQ Strategy. Jake's experience as a missionary kid will be either an asset or a liability to his overall CQ, depending on whether he exercises CQ Strategy.

When we seek to understand and question whether we truly understand, we begin to progress in using our cross-cultural experiences themselves as a way to nurture CQ Strategy. Hands-on experiences in different cultures are extremely effective ways to learn about cross-cultural dynamics and differences, especially when combined with CQ Strategy. There's benefit both to continued exposure to the same place and to a variety of experiences in many different contexts. If a person's CQ Strategy is high, multiple experiences in diverse settings yield some of the greatest growth in overall cultural intelligence.[4]

Don't limit your thinking about these kinds of immersions to the encounters that happen when you're on a short-term missions trip. Cross-cultural encounters abound all around us. Watch the Spanish channel for a while, eat at a Thai restaurant, attend the Irish festival in a nearby town, interview a nearby seasonal farming worker, or watch BBC news online. Few things aid us in developing CQ Strategy like cross-cultural encounters themselves.

One of the leading experts on the educational value of cross-cultural travel, Kenneth Cushner, writes, "Travel affords one to see the world from another perspective. But these lessons don't always jump right out at you. More often than not, they are missed because of one's inability to perceive what has gone on from the local perspective, or one's inability to step back from the situation."[5] We have to shut down our mental cruise control to benefit most from our travel abroad.

Don't miss the chance to use your short-term missions trip to see the world differently. Step back from a situation to interpret what's going on. That's what we're after with CQ Strategy. We're trying to reframe what we see and create new categories for understanding. In the short run, engaging in CQ Strategy can result in a far more healthy and redemptive short-term missions trip. In the long run, thinking more critically and carefully about what we observe can significantly transform the way we understand, interpret, and live out God's mission in the world. Surely that's worth the hard work of journaling, reading some good novels, and questioning our assumptions.

Most short-term missions trips occur in groups. Teams go together from churches, schools, and other organizations. A key component to team members being able to engage in CQ Strategy on a short-term missions trip is spending time on planning and reflection. Dialoguing with others about cues and their interpretation is a real asset to doing short-term missions in community rather than by oneself.

Back to Shanghai

No one in the group meandering through Shanghai seems to have a whole lot of CQ Strategy. Jake assumes his extended experience in Mexico makes him a natural. Overall, he's a confident guy who isn't very fazed by how he may come off to others, particularly in a vastly different world like China.

Sarah, the resident intercultural expert on the team, has just enough knowledge about cultures to make her dangerous. She seems to know all the answers but isn't aware or mindful enough to be able to interpret accurately what she's observing. As a result, her high CQ Knowledge, when not combined with high CQ Strategy, may actually hinder her effectiveness in China. This is something I've observed again and again. Pre-departure training can be vitally helpful in developing CQ Knowledge. When we fail to use it in tandem with CQ Strategy, however, it often results in worsened engagement cross-culturally than if we'd spent no time at all studying the cultural nuances. This is what my African friend Mark described to me in London when he said, "[Those North American youth pastors] have prepared just enough for this trip to make them dangerous." The goal is to grow in our cross-cultural understanding and then combine that with a thoughtful, reflective perspective.

Jenny gives us the most hope for CQ Strategy of anyone on the Shanghai team. She lacks the ability to interpret what she's observing, but she knows enough to stop herself and question what's really going on. With a heightened degree of CQ Knowledge through more interaction with Chinese people and by additional study about how cultures relate, Jenny will be well on her way toward cultural intelligence.

Join me in committing to work on CQ Strategy. As we learn to interpret, reflect on, and reframe our observations, we create a link between our cross-cultural understanding and the behavior we're after in our mission work. CQ Strategy helps connect our cultural knowledge with something deeper. Once we start down this road, we see an ever-growing window into life as a whole. Suddenly we have a new way of seeing and approaching our faith, our interactions with people, our family, and our life. Open your eyes! Wider! Once you get a glimpse of God's world this way, you'll never want to go back to life *without* cultural intelligence.

Strategies to Improve Your CQ Strategy

Anytime:

1. Notice. Don't respond. When you see something unusual, don't jump to conclusions. Stop and consider possible explanations.
2. Plan for ways to incorporate culturally diverse perspectives in the things you read and talk about.
3. Creatively seek feedback from individuals who come from various cultural backgrounds.

On Your Short-Term Trip:

1. What color do you notice more than any other today? Compare your observations with others.
2. Look for something that is different from home. What about something that looks the same?
3. Journal about the things you are observing and suggest possible explanations. But don't rush to conclusions. Check out your interpretations with someone from the culture.

12

Actions Speak Louder than Words

CQ Action

Jun flagged down a couple of taxis to get everyone from the university back to the hostel where they were staying. They had just finished their second day of teaching. Jake and Jun ended up in the same taxi together, so Jake used it as a chance to get some feedback from Jun. "So, Jun. How's it going, bro? Are we doing okay? Are you happy with the team?"

"Everything is okay," said Jun. "It's fine."

"Well, what's that supposed to mean?" asked Jake. "That's a very noncommittal answer. 'Okay'? 'Fine'? C'mon, bud. Shoot straight with me. How do you feel the team is doing?"

"It's okay, Jake. We will talk about it." Jun immediately started pointing out the Chongqing Harbor, where the Yangtze and Jialing Rivers meet.

Jake was a little frustrated by Jun's nondescript feedback, but he decided not to push it any farther. Instead, he feigned interest in the places Jun pointed out along the way.

Meanwhile, Mandy, one of the other team members, struck up a conversation with her taxi driver. His English impressed her. It turns out he had spent several years in Hong Kong. Knowing the prevalence of the British influence in Hong Kong, Mandy purposely used the hard *o* when she said the word *process*. She had some Canadian friends who always said it that way. She also said words like *library* really fast, as she had often heard Brits do. She referred to it as the "libree." As Jenny and Brian listened to her talk with the taxi driver, they began to laugh as she forced British pronunciations of English words.

Jenny, the ever-reflective one, wondered what Mandy was doing. *Is that really more effective than just speaking English the way we typically speak it? I wonder if it sounds as forced to this driver as it does to me.* Was Mandy's behavior a good demonstration of cultural intelligence? Is that what it looks like to be high in CQ Action?

The team got together to discuss their first two days of teaching. Jake, the infamous storyteller of the group, shared a few of his greatest blunders. Jenny, the ever-reflective one, bombarded Jun with questions: "Why won't anyone respond when I ask the group a question? Will I offend them if I ask them not to call me Miss Gilmore? Some of them are older than me! Should I try to make things more participative, or is it better for me to use the lecture-style that they seem more comfortable with? Or am I even right in assuming they're more comfortable with lecture?" For each of Jun's responses, Sarah, the cross-cultural expert, had her own two cents to throw in.

Once we improve our CQ Drive, Knowledge, and Strategy, can we behave in a way that demonstrates our love for Christ and others? That's what CQ Action is most concerned about.

What Is CQ Action?

CQ Action is the extent to which we change our verbal and nonverbal actions when interacting cross-culturally. Everything from how fast we talk to our topics of conversation are a part of CQ Action. Cultural taboos such as pointing or talking with our hands in our pockets are some of the behaviors avoided when observing CQ Action. CQ Action is being sensitive and appropriate with our actions and behavior as we engage in a new culture. The point isn't to act as chameleons wherever we go. Rather, in an attempt to relate to the people we meet, we strive to interact in meaningful and appropriate ways.

The other three capabilities of cultural intelligence are vitally important for all the reasons we've just explored. At the end of the day, however, our cultural intelligence and, more importantly, our short-term missions endeavors will be measured by our behavior. The things we actually say and do and the ways we go about our work become the litmus test for whether we're doing short-term missions with cultural intelligence. As we'll see shortly, the other three capabilities are essential in nurturing CQ Action, but cultural intelligence is not just a mind game of having the right motivation, gathering information, and learning how to interpret cues. Eventually, we have to act and engage. Our ability to draw on what we learn from the other three capabilities to act appropriately is CQ Action.

The biggest problems for most short-term missions teams are not technical or administrative. The biggest challenges lie in communication, misunderstanding, personality conflicts, poor leadership, and bad teamwork. These are all parts of CQ Action. The difference between short-term trips done with CQ Action and those done without is significant. Short-term missions trips without CQ Action look more like a typical tourist experience. The tour group sticks together as a group of outsiders, stays in cushy places, seldom veers into the local cuisine, and views the culture as a sporting event rather than actually playing the game.

An important part of CQ Action is seeing the ways behaviors can have different meanings in different places. Behaviors such as laughing, shouting, smiling, and talking quietly are some universal behaviors we share as humans. However, culture programs our minds to interpret those behaviors differently. Smiling is expected in certain situations and assumed to mean certain things in one place but has entirely different uses elsewhere. Nudity is crude in public and intimate in private for most North Americans, but it has very different meanings in many tribal cultures. Students sitting still and nodding their heads can mean something entirely different in one culture as compared to the next.

An individual with high CQ Action is not necessarily someone who masters all the unique habits and behaviors of every culture visited. That's next to impossible, especially during brief immersions such as short-term missions trips. Instead, flexibility and adjustment are the crucial components that accompany CQ Action. A person high in CQ Action will use nonverbal cues as a silent language to learn in various places and will be careful not to quickly assign meanings. The goal is to reduce misunderstanding and communicate respect more than it is to mimic others' behavior.

Behaving in a way that's culturally intelligent is clearly easier said than done. For years I've understood theoretically that it's not uncommon for men in many cultures to hold hands with other men without it meaning anything beyond a display of friendship. I've often explained this phenomenon to other people as a clear example of our need to beware of making quick judgments based on the same behavior in our culture. It was another thing, however, when I was walking down the streets of Chiang Rai, Thailand, and John, an Akha man, slipped his hand around my waist. He put his hand in my left rear pocket as a North American high school boy might do with his girlfriend. John left his hand there as we walked for several blocks. I desperately wanted to pull away. It was one thing to read about such behavior in a sterile environment back home; it was quite another to experience it while walking through the streets of Chiang Rai. So what does it look like for us to nurture CQ in the ways that we behave on our short-term missions experiences?

Nurturing CQ Action

Many resources are devoted to helping us act appropriately when we travel cross-culturally. Several authors give helpful information about the kinds of gifts to avoid giving. We're told how to entertain, gestures to avoid, how to exchange business cards, and the kinds of greetings to use. "Don't point. Never pay with your left hand. Kiss both cheeks. Don't hug. Be sure to use her formal title." The lists are endless. If we move to a culture for several years, we may be able to master many of these behaviors, but what does it look like when we move in and out of different cultures all the time? There are several things to consider in nurturing CQ Action.

See CQ Action as the Outcome

At the risk of being redundant, the most important way to nurture CQ Action is to nurture the other three CQ capabilities: drive, knowledge, and strategy. This is the irony. The success of our short-term projects is judged mostly by our behavior because actions demonstrate most clearly whether or not we're culturally intelligent. However, trying to change our behavior itself is the least effective way of nurturing CQ. Our actions are so ingrained into our habits that it takes far more than a book or several training sessions to teach us CQ Action.

However, as we nurture the other aspects of CQ, they have inevitable implications for how we behave. In a sense, CQ Action is the outcome of the other three CQ capabilities. For example, CQ Drive will help align our motivation with doing the hard work that comes with interacting as an outsider in a new place. We can use CQ Knowledge to understand the different ways cultures approach power distance; this will inform how we interact with people of different status. And CQ Strategy will help us tune in to the cues coming from our interactions and organize those cues within our growing sense of cultural intelligence as a whole. These work together toward helping us adjust our behavior.

Some of our behaviors can be modified and manipulated, but most of our energy should be placed on the other three capabilities of CQ. CQ Action is perhaps the most helpful way to expose our need for cultural intelligence. As we seek to change our behavior, we don't have access to each other's thoughts, feelings, or motivation. We can rely only on what we see and hear in others' verbal, vocal, facial, and other bodily expressions. Nurturing our CQ Drive, Knowledge, and Strategy is the best way to make behavior changes.

Practice

There is, however, value in practicing some basic habits used in various cultures to make them part of our behavioral repertoire. For example, because people in so many places where I travel consider it offensive to hand someone something with the left hand, even when I'm home, I often try to avoid using my left hand. Ninety-nine percent of the people with whom I interact in the United States don't give a second thought to whether they receive my change at the cash register from my right hand or my left hand. However, I want it to be second nature for me to use my right hand to avoid offending an Arab acquaintance.

I speak very fast, especially when I teach or preach. This is another area where I have to practice—slowing down. Frankly, many of my North American audiences would be happy if I'd slow down a bit when I speak. When I speak overseas, I often do so with people who speak English as a second language or where an interpreter is translating on my behalf. Because my rate of speech is so ingrained in how I communicate, I have to work hard to slow down. It takes a lot of effort and writing all over my notes "slow down." But these are the kinds of things we can work on to improve the way we behave. Practice. Practice. Practice.

Adaptability

Some of us are naturals at interacting socially with people, even if they're complete strangers. We find it easy to initiate conversations, listen to others, and bring other people into the conversation. Others struggle desperately to master a conversation. Having a natural ability socially can be a real help cross-culturally, but we must beware of thinking we can rely on those natural skills when interacting with someone from a different cultural background. The very thing that breaks the ice with someone in our own culture could be irrelevant or offensive in another. Appropriate topics for small talk, humor, and even if and how we should ask questions are all things deeply impacted by our cultural background. We often need to develop new social skills to interact effectively in new cultural contexts. This is one of many reasons why the most important characteristic to develop for CQ Action is adaptability.

As we learn to become adaptable and flexible, we'll gain the CQ Action needed to interact with unique individuals and in unique situations. The challenge lies in gaining some general skills of adaptability so that we can adapt instantly to specific people, cultures, and circumstances. "Cross-cultural skills are not fixed routines but flexible abilities that can—with the guidance of mindfulness—be modified to meet new or changing conditions."[1] The challenge is to expand our repertoire of skilled behaviors needed in different places and knowing how to use them. The skilled routines we master in one culture may be counterproductive in another, to the extent that we have to "unlearn" them in a new situation. Again, this is why adaptability is crucial to CQ Action.

As in several of these areas, some cultures program individuals to be better at this than others. For example, cultures that feel less threatened by uncertainty—such as Indians, Brits, and Jamaicans—typically achieve CQ Action more easily. In addition, learning to be adaptable is directly connected to our CQ Strategy. It's a part of the interpretive process in which we learn to read cues and change our plans based on what seems to work and what doesn't. Having a plan so we don't fly by the seat of our pants is an integral part of interacting with CQ Action, but just as essential is the process of holding to those plans loosely and being willing to toss them in a split second when necessary.

And once again, cross-cultural experiences themselves are one of the best ways to improve our adaptability. Cultural blunders are inevitable. That's okay. Grace abounds. Just use the mistakes as a way to improve the way you interact in future cross-cultural encounters so that you don't keep repeating the same mistakes. As we persevere through the continual challenges confronting us in cross-cultural communication and interaction and gain understanding about cultural values to reframe our assumptions, we begin to behave more appropriately and effectively.

Behavioral Training

Many of the short-term missions training tools that exist focus on building CQ Knowledge and Action. Continue to use the valuable techniques offered by many of these resources. The key challenge lies at the point of applying and integrating the material to what you will actually do on your cross-cultural experience. Find ways to use role-playing or, better yet, real-life cross-cultural immersions closer to home rather than simply studying material theoretically in the fellowship hall of your church.

One of the most effective ways to train yourself and your short-term team in CQ Action is through exposure to uncomfortable situations. For example, you could begin having a conversation about the challenges of CQ Action by walking up to a friend and purposely violating her personal space. Keep within two inches of her face, and as she backs away from you, keep moving with her. Have the whole group try this with each other. Or suddenly put your hand on your friend's shoulder and leave it there as you talk. Or talk in a way that eliminates nonverbal expressions as much as possible. Or choose an unusual, unfamiliar food and insist that everyone eat it. These kinds of experiences help to train people in CQ Action. More than anything, they help reveal the need for CQ as a whole.

It's easy to speak confidently about our ability to act appropriately, but when we become uncomfortable, it's another thing to act appropriately. As a result, one of the most significant times for developing CQ Action is when we first enter a new culture and when we first return home. These are our most pivotal learning times. The first impressions and the immediate dissonance experienced both in leaving home and coming back are filled with opportunities for learning adaptability. Be sure to check out the cross-cultural training resources listed in the appendix for more guidance on training for effective cross-cultural behavior.

Back to Shanghai

Jake is a natural conversationalist. He can talk to complete strangers on the street and put them at ease. The highly relational context of Mexico where he grew up has really helped him be a natural leader and networker most places he's been. So far, however, he doesn't seem to have connected with Jun. In particular, he violated the social practices of Chinese culture when he asked Jun for a direct evaluation and assessment in the midst of a very informal setting—riding in a taxi. Jun just wasn't going to go there. He gave Jake a very indirect, seemingly ambiguous response. Jake knew what it would mean if he had been the one saying, "It's okay" or "It's fine." That would be code language for "I'm not very impressed" or "It's okay *but . . .*"

Meanwhile, Mandy wants so hard to speak appropriately that she's trying to use British-style pronunciation rather than just saying words as an American would. What she doesn't realize, however, is that her attempts at acting appropriately may in fact have the opposite effect. The taxi driver could easily be insulted. Why does Mandy think he isn't smart enough to figure out what she means when she pronounces words the way she typically would? Inevitably, the taxi driver has seen lots of American television and movies throughout his years in Hong Kong and now in Shanghai. Does he really need Mandy to force herself to pronounce words differently?

Actions speak louder than words. This cliché, though overused, really applies here. Most of the short-term participants I studied said the right things before going to a new culture. They demonstrated a desire to learn, they realized they may come off as loud and brash, and they were well aware of their shortcomings when it came to cross-cultural work. Yet when they actually went on their trips, much of their behavior didn't line up with what they had said.

Our tendency is to use all our energy to change our behavior, but we can't possibly anticipate the endless situations and encounters that will arise. Therefore, the full-orbed approach of CQ is essential to getting our actions to speak a message that reflects God's glory through our postures, behaviors, and dispositions.

Strategies to Improve Your CQ Action

Anytime:

1. Observe and record verbal and nonverbal behaviors you see in individuals from different cultures.
2. Practice new behaviors that come from various cultures.
3. Adapt how you ask for feedback, write an email, or give instructions based on how you would do so with people from different cultures.

On Your Short-Term Trip:

1. Create a list of taboos. Avoid them.
2. Do a behavior as the locals would. Practice adapting. Just be careful not to be offensive.
3. Go through a day and imagine what life would be like if you lived here. Empathize.

13

The Heart of the Matter

Shema

Perhaps you're thinking, *Cultural intelligence, CQ Strategy, power distance—does it have to be so complicated? I just want to love people in Romania!* Or maybe you're thinking, Forget it! You've convinced me that so many problems occur with short-term missions that I'm going to boycott the whole deal.

I hope you don't come to either conclusion. I understand the tension. Surely we don't want to make missions so complicated that you need a PhD in intercultural studies to succeed, but neither do we want to explain away the many challenges of our past mistakes.

At the end of the day, cultural intelligence helps us do what we were created to do: participate with God in making the world a better place. Missions is at the very core of our calling. In my mind, missions isn't something that started after Adam and Eve sinned, and it's not just about getting souls saved. It's about living in light of our creation as image bearers of God. Missions—short-term, long-term, overseas, next-door—is about giving people a living picture of who God is, what God cares about, and how God acts. Acting on God's behalf was Adam and Eve's purpose long before sin entered the picture.

Missions Began with Adam and Eve

Paul is often described as being the first missionary. Others think of the disciples as the first missionaries, and still others go as far back as Abraham. My understanding of missions, however, is rooted all the way back in Adam and Eve. They were the first humans called by God to work as agents of God. Long before sin corrupted the earth, ages before churches painted Matthew 28 on banners for mission conferences, Adam and Eve were created to represent God in the world, and therefore, our ultimate identity lies in our missional calling.

Missions is rooted in creation. It's not simply a corrective to sin. It's what God created us to do as human beings. Adam and Eve were created to care for the animals and the garden as God would. They were to creatively develop their surroundings. God told them to be fruitful and multiply and to show their children and grandchildren the cares and ways of God. Adam and Eve were to reflect God's glory with every word and deed. God called them to be priests over all creation—to represent God to creation and creation to God.

Though Adam and Eve failed at their mission, the invitation to God's people continued. The nation of Israel was created by God to be a priestly nation to the other nations. They were to give the other nations a picture of what Yahweh's nation looked like. Israel was created to be a nation that would bless the other nations. They were to act on God's behalf among the Gentiles.

Though Israel failed, God's invitation to the people of God continued. He divided the priestly nation into twelve tribes, and the levitical tribe became the priestly tribe. Notice the narrowing impact to which God was calling the people of God. Adam and Eve were given a priestly role among all creation, Israel to the rest of the nations, and Aaron and his sons to the nation of Israel, to intercede on their behalf with God. As they failed in accurately reflecting who God is, the scope of impact they were invited to make kept getting smaller.[1] (See fig. 2.)

Even the levitical priests failed in their priestly calling, but God's redemptive plan continued. Jesus, the second Adam, came as the perfect priest and sacrifice all in one. God became one of us in part so that we could see how we were intended to live. Christ was the epitome of cultural intelligence by giving us the most accessible and understandable

Figure 2

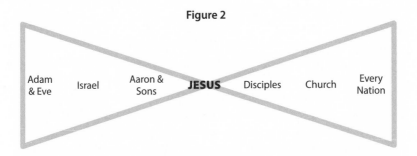

Adam & Eve | Israel | Aaron & Sons | **JESUS** | Disciples | Church | Every Nation

picture of how the first Adam was intended to live. It's within that long history of missions that Jesus declares, "Go and make disciples of *all* nations" (Matt. 28:19, emphasis added). Everything in the story changes. And we're invited to extend God's reign among people everywhere.

Jesus's disciples obeyed the Great Commission by establishing the church. Peter refers to the church as the "priesthood" of believers (1 Pet. 2:9). As part of the church, we're to live out the priestly mission that has been upon the people of God throughout history. Just as Adam and Eve, Israel, and the disciples were called to extend God's reign, so also are we. Short-term missions trips are a way for us to join with a long legacy of God's people in making God known to all the world.[2]

God has continually called us as a special people to be engaged in missions. We don't have the prerogative of either extreme: "Who cares about all that CQ stuff; I just want to serve!" or "I'm going to boycott the whole missions thing. There's too much baggage." Missions is what we're created to do—together. So we must figure out how to keep improving our obedience to God's invitation and call.

If missions is what we were created to do, and if we're to be the physical presence of Christ in the world, then working on how to best embody Christ to the world should be of prime importance—that's the essence of cultural intelligence. CQ is more than just an interesting model for talking about cross-cultural effectiveness. It's a way to enhance how we live out our eternal mission as people—to reflect God's glory to the world. It's more than just a tool for short-term missions trips. It's a pathway for helping us live out our mission as we encounter people from different cultures every day—at the airport, at school, at work, on the phone, in the grocery store, and online.

What Matters Most?

As we live out Christ's presence in the world, we need to remember what Jesus considered to be the most important commandment: "Love God, love others." Everything else rises and falls on this.

This was Jesus's reply when the teacher of the law asked him, "Teacher, which is the greatest commandment in the Law?" (Matt. 22:36). Jesus's response wasn't random. He quoted something he had been reciting since his childhood—a portion of the Shema from the Old Testament. *Shema* means "to listen" or "to hear." To a Jew, the Shema was as familiar as the song "Jesus Loves Me" is to many of us today. The Shema was one of those phrases children recited when they were young, and they never forgot it.

Jesus's reference to the Shema helps us live out our mission—whether in our everyday lives at home or during a two-week mission trip. He brings us back to what God's people were called to do throughout the Old Testament. For several centuries, day after day, year after year, the people of God recited the Shema as a continual reminder of what mattered most as they lived out their mission. The Shema was to be embraced in their hearts, impressed upon their children, and declared to all who encountered them both in word and in deed (Deut. 6).

This daily practice of reciting the Shema continued during Jesus's day. He grew up reciting it with Mary and Joseph at home and in the nearby synagogues. The followers of God declared it every day during Jesus's childhood as a way to acknowledge their allegiance to God alone. To recite the Shema was to wholeheartedly accept the kingdom of God in their lives.

Paul also declared the centrality of the Shema to living out the mission of God. Paul frequently referenced the priorities of loving God and loving others as he ministered for several decades after Jesus ascended to heaven. All his letters include both emphases.

The purpose of enhancing our cultural intelligence is to become better at loving God and loving others. As we persevere through the challenges that come with interacting cross-culturally, we demonstrate a love that reflects God's glory. As we understand the people God has made in cultures all over the world, we're drawn to worship. As we behave in ways that set others at ease and respect their differences, we give people glimpses of Jesus. That's why CQ is so vital. It's not about simply being more successful at cross-cultural work; it's a way to move us forward in expressing God's love to people everywhere.

As soon as we lose sight of the Shema, we risk doing short-term missions for ourselves rather than for the sake of those we're serving—or God. Self-serving missions can be described as "Christian 'parachuting,' a decontextualized 'dropping in' to a needy situation just long enough to distribute beneficial goods that sometimes places unwanted stress on a beleaguered community."[3] These kinds of so-called mission trips are more like sightseeing than genuine service and ministry to a group of people. We cannot truly serve those we do not know and love. However, as we enter into deep relationships with those we serve, we, in a small way like Jesus, take on others' burdens as our own and begin to truly lay down our lives so that those we serve may encounter the life of Jesus.[4]

Love for people and love for God have to drive our short-term missions work. That happens only as short-term missions experiences become part of a lifelong journey of seeking to love people cross-culturally, whenever and wherever we encounter them.

We've covered a lot of ground in our journey together. My hope is that you won't be discouraged from engaging in cross-cultural settings because of the many pitfalls exposed. Instead, continue to pursue cross-cultural opportunities to live out God's mission and do so with your eyes wide open. I want to conclude by reviewing several things to consider as we serve with eyes wide open.

Ten Starting Points for Doing Short-Term Missions with Cultural Intelligence

1. Realize That God's a Lot Bigger than Your Short-Term Missions Trip

God's sovereignty above and beyond our mission trips should be a word of encouragement to some and a word of caution to others. Our North American sense of urgency can cause us to think God's work around the world is entirely dependent on our short-term missions projects. God graciously allows us to be a part of extending divine redemption around the world. But countless others are part of that as well. When we're discouraged, may we be reminded that God has had thousands of years of turning our most feeble attempts at missions into beautiful reflections of God's glory. When we're tempted to overstate our role, may we be reminded that only God can turn a heart of stone into a heart of flesh. Only God can use a group of twenty people holding Romanian babies to be a part of what gives those babies a real-life experience of Jesus. In the words of Jonathan Edwards, at the end of the day, "God's work of power and grace will not be thwarted by our great many errors and sin."[5]

2. Stop Petting the Poor

Whenever possible, find a way to connect your short-term projects to long-term, interdependent relationships. Dropping into a food shelter once a year at Thanksgiving or making random mission trips that get us more stamps in our passports don't keep the Shema at the forefront of missions. To love people is to get involved in their lives. That's messy and complicated. Let's persevere through the hard work of hanging in there with the same group of people rather than blowing in and out of a lot of different places. When you go, sit down with people and hear their stories. Share your story—not just the shiny, testimony-material parts of your story but also the parts that reveal your weaknesses.

The North American church has things to share. The majority world church has things to share. The North American church has needs. The majority world church has needs. Let's move beyond demeaning relationships that put us in positions of power and move toward interdependent, loving relationships in which we meet one another's needs.

Here's what some African church leaders said when asked what they wanted most to say to North American churches: "Please raise our dignity before the Christians and citizens of North America. We are not naive, backward, and ignorant black people. Instead, we are your brothers and sisters in the family of God who are seeking to be faithful to his calling on our lives."

Initiatives such as the one led by Chip Huber at Wheaton Academy give us a positive example of short-term missions done with a heart to benefit both the goers and the receivers. Huber describes the long-term relationships Wheaton Academy high school students have been developing with some of the Zamtran people in Zambia. It's a great picture of affluent, Chicago suburbanites engaging in missions *with* passionate, prayer-dependent Zambians. The Chicago students sacrificed time and money to raise more than $225,000 to battle AIDS among the Zamtran people; Zamtran believers sacrificed time and money to host the American students and taught them what it means to pray sacrificially. The Zamtrans blessed the Americans, and the Americans blessed the Zamtrans. Together they discerned before God what it looked like to be a blessing among the nations, particularly among AIDS victims and their families.[6] Long-term commitments to do missions interdependently and cross-culturally are extending the reign of God.

3. Be Yourself

The tension we've considered throughout this journey is to understand cross-cultural differences enough to adapt and act appropriately without trying to be someone we aren't. Serving with eyes wide open means seeing yourself and others in a new light and making appropriate changes to who you are and how you relate. But it's not about trying to be like whomever you're with. Sometimes North Americans react to the criticisms of majority world pastors by bashing all that's North American. It can be tempting to deprecate everything Western as a way to gain credibility with non-Westerners, but that's inauthentic and an overreaction. There are some wonderful things about being Westerners and North Americans, and while we have plenty to redeem in our culture, the point is not to run from the culture of which we're a part.

4. Try, Try Again

Don't be so discouraged by the critiques in this book that you don't get involved at all. Persevere through the conflicting perspectives you observe by using CQ Drive. I've been in cross-cultural settings where I apologized for my North American perspective so much while teaching that it became laborious for my students. I understated the value I could bring by saying I was merely there to facilitate discussion, to which my host privately countered, "We did not bring you all the way here just to facilitate our discussion. Teach!" We need to keep our awareness on high alert as we seek to gather and interpret cues and acknowledge our limitations given our cultural programming. Then we need to teach with conviction and passion. Don't allow the challenges of cross-cultural differences to make you so overly tentative and apologetic that you come off as timid and uncertain.

Without question, my hardest weeks of work are those I spend in a new place trying to navigate a new set of cultural values and assumptions. Cross-cultural work is not for the weary. The excitement of new sights and sounds wears off pretty quickly. But as we persevere through the inevitable conflict and dissonance, we will reap the rewards of seeing ourselves, others, and God in renewed ways.

5. Seek to Understand

Prepare for your short-term trip by enhancing your CQ Knowledge. Spend time learning about the cultural differences you'll encounter in the specific place you're going. If possible, talk with others who have been where you're going and, best of all, interact with people from the culture itself. Use your short-term trip to improve your overall understanding of cross-cultural differences. Allow your growing understanding to give you an enhanced perspective on what occurs in cross-cultural situations without having a Sarah-like, know-it-all approach.

6. On Second Thought—Think Again!

Question your assumptions. Question your assumptions. Question your assumptions. If this book has done nothing else, I hope it's helped you rethink your assumptions about short-term work. CQ Strategy sounds technical, but it's simply slowing down our activity long enough so we can look at what's going on below the surface. Work on this during your next short-term trip. Practice it when you encounter someone from another culture in the next week or so. When you're inclined to make an assumption about that person or you hear someone else do so, stop and consider whether it's an accurate assumption. Don't be too quick to jump to conclusions. Turn off the mental cruise control.

Question your assumptions about why you're doing a mission trip in the first place (motivation). Question your assumptions about what's urgent and what isn't (urgency). Question your assumptions about how much the people you're going to encounter are like you (common ground). Question your assumptions about what's biblical (the Bible). Question your assumptions about how happy people are who make two dollars a day (money). Last but not least, question your assumptions when you begin to jump to either/or categories (simplicity). We'll make a lot of strides in embodying an accurate picture of Jesus when we step back and question our assumptions.

7. Realize That Actions Speak Louder than Words

Eventually, we must move beyond conceptualizing cross-cultural work and go for it through CQ Action. Mistakes are inevitable. Use your actions as a way to assess whether you're spending enough time in the other three dimensions of CQ, since those three are the best ways to enhance CQ Action. Few things will help you grow in those areas like actually encountering people and lifestyles in a different setting. I teach intercultural courses in many different settings, but I'm well aware that classroom content can only do so much to enhance cultural intelligence. There's no substitute for being immersed in actual cross-cultural situations.

If you're part of a group on a short-term trip, allow regular time throughout the experience to process what's occurring by way of intercultural behavior. Find someone from the culture, preferably your host, to be a "cultural interpreter" for you. Don't just spend all your time with your fellow teammates or with Western missionaries. Finally, don't miss out on the value of the lessons that can be learned after returning home. Commit to investing in something more than a picture-sharing party. Find ongoing ways to process the lessons learned as a way to enhance your CQ Action in future interactions cross-culturally. Read this book again after you come home. See how your perspective has changed since the first time you read it.

8. *Give Up Trying to See Who's In and Who's Out*

Sharing Christ with people is a core part of most short-term missions projects—whether through verbal presentations of the gospel or projects that tangibly embody elements of the gospel, such as medical clinics or relief work. While taking our Christian calling seriously, we need to be freed from trying to figure out who's "in" as a member of the people of God and who's "out." I'm not suggesting we go easy on calling people to follow Jesus. Every one of our encounters, every day, should include a call to our fellow human beings to follow Christ—whether the call comes implicitly or explicitly.

I often talk with short-termers who are confused about which religious groups they should consider close enough to our faith that they can assume people in that movement are genuine believers. Or they want a list of the groups whose followers are "out." I'm really not interested in going there, because it's far too risky for me to think I can ever know God's final judgment on another person, particularly if I determine that solely in light of their religious affiliation. In the words of missiologist Leslie Newbigin, "I do not claim to know in advance [a person's] ultimate destiny. I meet the person simply as a witness, as one who has been laid hold of by [Christ] and placed in a position where I can only point to Jesus as the one who can make sense of the whole human situation that [we share] as human beings."[7] I'm to love God and love others and leave up to God what only God can do: rescue souls.

9. *Incorporate Short-Term Missions as Part of Your Everyday Life*

Serving with eyes wide open means not only asking the deeper, reflective questions evoked by CQ Strategy but also placing them within the full scope of our lives as yet another way of living out our Christian calling. We best not reduce the priesthood of believers or our obedience to the Great Commission just to short-term missions. If we do, most of us get to engage in missions only a couple weeks a year at best, maybe only once in a lifetime, and for people like my parents, never! Short-term missions can be part of the Great Commission and of living out our priestly role—*part* of it!

Don't go running overseas to do something you aren't already doing in your own neighborhood. If you want to fight for justice in the brothels of Cambodia, start by being an agent of justice in your home and at work. If you want to share Jesus with children in a Romanian orphanage, don't neglect the children playing at the park around the corner from your house. If you have a heart to use your business skills to help people in Uzbekistan create wealth, think about how your business practices in your suburban office have global implications.

I could go on and on. My book *What Can I Do: Making a Global Difference Right Where You Are* is specifically devoted to this topic. Teachers can introduce students to global issues from their suburban classrooms, computer wizards can develop software that serves people in places around the world, and musicians can compose pieces that reflect God's glory—all of these are part of living out our Christian calling in an increasingly multicultural world. Short-term missions is just another opportunity for us to live out what we need to be living 24/7 wherever we are.

As we've seen many times throughout the last few chapters, CQ is not something we master before our next mission trip. It's a lifelong journey of wrestling with what it means to use our finances, our gifts, our connections, and our time to extend God's reign among all the nations. As we grow in our CQ, our short-term missions trips will be a more effective part of God's work in the world and will help us live out God's mission—whether we're in a cubicle in Midwest America or swinging a hammer in Namibia.[8]

10. Love God, Love Others

More than anything else, "'Love the Lord your God with all your heart and with all your soul and with all your mind.' This is the first and greatest commandment. And the second is like it: 'Love your neighbor as yourself'" (Matt. 22:37–39).

When you get up and when you go to sleep, love God, love others. When you travel on vacation and when you travel as part of a mission team, love God, love others. When you encounter an immigrant and when you overhear a foreign language, love God, love others. The essence of serving with eyes wide open is gaining cultural intelligence so we can more effectively reflect God to people who are culturally different from us.

A Checklist for Serving with Eyes Wide Open

Since the first edition of this book was released, a great deal of my research has moved toward asking, What does effective short-term missions look like? After taking a good, hard look at the criticisms, I'm far more interested in examining what we *should* do rather than what we're doing poorly. The following checklist stems from some of the most recent research on effective short-term missions and cross-cultural engagement. Most points apply specifically to leaders and organizers of short-term teams, but even those going on individual trips can benefit from many of them.

Designing the Trip

Before You Go

- Define the objective. Be clear on what you're trying to accomplish. Do this together with your partners on the receiving end. Ask what's needed and then ask again and again and again. You may need another organization to help you discern what's most needed in a local community or ministry. Be clear about what it is you're trying to accomplish for everyone involved.
- Commit to life change for everyone who participates (senders, goers, receivers).
- Plan the trip in light of the objective.
- Make sure your trip is part of a long-term plan for everyone involved (goers and receivers).
- Don't do there what you aren't doing at home. If you're going to teach English, teach English to immigrants at home. If you're going to work with children, don't overlook the children who need help in your own community. It doesn't always have to be a one-for-one connection, but be sure you haven't neglected the needs right in your own backyard.

- Recruit leaders in light of the objective. The leaders of your trip will make the biggest difference in whether you do culturally intelligent short-term missions or not. It's inevitable that the team participants will have a variety of motivations, but the motivation of the leaders is what matters most.
- Publicize the trip and recruit participants in light of the objective.
- Realize that smaller groups are usually more effective. The larger the group, the harder it is to engage with the local culture. Staying in locals' homes is best when possible. That's next to impossible with a large group. Less than seven is an ideal number.
- Remind participants of the objective.
- Require a post-trip commitment from the participants upfront (e.g., "Part of this trip requires participating in a debrief program for three to six months upon your return").
- Give top priority to leadership orientation. Leaders are the ones who most need to understand the potential challenges and opportunities. Expose them to cultural intelligence so they can effectively guide the team members.
- Prepare. Conduct orientation sessions for your team and discuss with your partners how the receivers will be prepared. Emphasize the necessary spiritual posture and learn what questions to ask to learn about the culture and God's work there.
- Assess your CQ. Take the *Short-Term Missions CQ Assessment* not as a condition for who can be involved but to get everyone reflecting more specifically on the cross-cultural aspects of the experience. (See www.culturalQ.com for information.)

During the Trip

- Remind participants of the objective. In the midst of serving, it's easy to lose sight of the primary objective.
- Do missions with the local believers. Don't do missions "to" people or "for" people. Do it together.
- Worship and fellowship with the locals. Many groups report that bonding with their team from home is a highlight of their

experience. I understand that. But don't miss the rich experience of having regular times of worship and, if possible, studying the Scriptures with local Christians. Develop new friendships and bonds.

- Consider the four capabilities of CQ daily. Use the cultural intelligence model as a basic framework to guide your cultural engagement: How's our motivation? What do we need to learn about the culture? How should we plan? How should we adapt?

- Debrief on the fly. In addition to daily team debriefings, don't miss some of the most transformative times to debrief with another team member, such as while driving away from an afternoon at the dump.

After the Trip

- Remind participants of the objective.

- Emphasize learning transfer. What have we learned that we don't want to forget? How should this change my life at home?

- Emphasize the good and the bad. Look for ways to describe the locals and their culture to those back home in terms of both the needs you observed and the things that are going well.

- Assess your CQ again. Compare your CQ scores with what they were before you left. Look at how to continue to grow in cultural intelligence so you can effectively communicate Christ's love across cultures at home too.

- Conduct an action-oriented debrief. Move beyond simply having a picture party. In light of what you've seen, what can you do? For some, it may mean raising money to help with a need they saw. Others may want to organize a prayer team or create an awareness initiative. Others may decide they want to begin teaching English to local immigrants. For some, it may mean a career change. Do short-term missions with a long-term view. A two-thousand-dollar trip is a lot of money if you just go paint a wall for ten days, but it's a valuable investment if it creates a long-term role in meeting some of the needs observed—at home and abroad.

Conclusion

How does our lack of cultural intelligence diminish our attempts to love God and love others? That's the heart of the matter.

Open your eyes. Can you see what you missed before? The challenges for doing short-term missions well are huge. But they pale in light of the guarantee that God *will* call people from every nation, tribe, language, and people group. I wrote this book because I want to change the way we think about and do short-term missions.

We began in chapter 1 with a sobering description of the needs of the world. Your short-term missions trip to Mexico next summer may seem like an insignificant drop in the sea of these needs. But when you see your trip in light of God's work across several millennia, it can be a valuable part of a worldwide revolution that can never be stopped.

Open your eyes. Can you see it? There's a worldwide revolution going on among God's people, and there has been ever since Adam and Eve. Despite the countless failures of God's people, God's reign continues to be extended all over the world. The church of Jesus Christ is growing faster than ever before. When we're part of the people of God, we're part of a worldwide revolution. We don't do short-term missions because we're shamed into it or because we're looking for something to do over spring break. We do it to join God in his worldwide revolution. Never before has Revelation 7:9 seemed more viable.

Can you see it? Can you see what John saw? Stranded out on the remote island of Patmos, the apostle John said, "There before me was a great multitude that no one could count, from every nation, tribe, people and language, standing before the throne and before the Lamb" (Rev. 7:9). It's going to happen. People from *every* nation will gather at the feet of Jesus, worshiping him. We get to be part of making that happen, along with the rest of God's people spread across the globe.

I pray you'll take the challenge to embark on a lifelong journey of cultural intelligence so that you might love others better and in turn grow in your love for Christ. May the world never look the same as a result of your resolve to serve with eyes wide open.

Appendix

Recommended Resources

On Poverty and Development

Easterly, William Russell. *The White Man's Burden: Why the West's Efforts to Aid the Rest Have Done So Much Ill and So Little Good.* New York: Penguin, 2007. A thorough critique by one of the foremost economists on Western efforts to get involved in international development.

Fikkert, Brian, and Steve Corbett. *When Helping Hurts: How to Alleviate Poverty without Hurting the Poor . . . and Yourself.* Chicago: Moody, 2012. An examination of Christian efforts to respond to poverty, including short-term missions and microenterprise development.

On Short-Term Missions Materials

Dearborn, Tim. *Short-Term Missions Workbook: From Mission Tourists to Global Citizens.* Downers Grove, IL: InterVarsity Press, 2003. A devotional to help guide participants through the life-changing possibilities of short-term missions experiences.

Gudgel, Brent. *Missio Docs: Mexico.* www.brentgudgel.com/doc-on-the-effectiveness-of-short-term-missions. A video documentary on

Azusa Pacific University's Mexico Outreach that exposes some of the critiques described in this book.

Mack, J., and Leeann Stiles. *Mack and Leeann's Guide to Short-term Mission*. Downers Grove, IL: Moody, 2000. An extremely practical guide for planning the logistics of a trip, including checklists, safety guidelines, getting the right documents together, and so on.

Powell, Kara, and Brad Griffin. *Deep Justice Journeys*. Short-term missions curriculum for youth ministries (includes material for before, during, and after the trip with both a leader's guide and a student workbook).

Round Trip Video Curriculum and Leader's Guide. DVD documentary/curriculum based on two churches that exchange missions trips—one in North Carolina and one in Kenya.

Standards of Excellence in Short-Term Missions. www.soe.org. Standards developed by a group of ministry leaders for doing short-term missions more effectively. The website includes a number of additional resources.

On Cultural Intelligence

The Cultural Intelligence Center. Devoted to ongoing research and development in the field of cultural intelligence. Information about research, assessments, and certification programs are available at www.culturalQ.com.

Livermore, David. *Cultural Intelligence: Improving Your CQ to Engage Our Multicultural World*. Grand Rapids: Baker Academic, 2009. A deeper and broader application of cultural intelligence to various forms of Christian ministry, including short-term missions, long-term missions, and local churches reaching out to culturally diverse communities

———. *The Cultural Intelligence Difference: Master the One Skill You Can't Do Without in Today's Global Economy*. New York: AMACOM, 2011. Written for a broader audience, this book provides a quick overview of CQ and is packed with dozens of proven strategies for improving the four CQ capabilities. Purchase of the physical book also includes access to the CQ online assessment.

On Long-Term Impact

Livermore, David. *What Can I Do: Making a Global Difference Right Where You Are*. Grand Rapids: Zondervan, 2011. Practical ideas for how Christians can make a world of difference from home. This book provides a way to translate a short-term missions experience into a lifetime of engagement in global missions through stories of Christians in business, retail, art, science, health care, and more. It also includes a discernment process for understanding how and where to get involved individually and as a ministry.

———, and Terry Linhart. *What Can We Do: Practical Ways Your Youth Ministry Can Have a Global Conscience*. Grand Rapids: Zondervan, 2011. Written primarily for youth ministry leaders who are looking for ways their youth ministry can be involved globally beyond the short-term missions trip. This book includes an overview of nine global issues and practical ways to teach them to students. The book offers many practical ways to get involved immediately.

Notes

Introduction

1. With apologies to my fellow "Americans" who share the American continents with me from Chile to Canada, I've chosen to use the term *American* as it's often used throughout the world—to describe people who are from the United States of America. I've done so for ease in writing and reading. However, I am sympathetic to the idea that the United States is but one country within the Americas!

2. Roger Peterson, Gordon Aeschliman, and R. Wayne Sneed, *Maximum Impact, Short-Term Mission: The God-Commanded Repetitive Deployment of Swift, Temporary Nonprofessional Missionaries* (Minneapolis: STEM, 2003).

3. *Colonialism* refers to a nation exerting its power over places outside its own boundaries. For example, nearly every country in places such as Africa and Southeast Asia was colonized throughout the eighteenth and nineteenth centuries (or before). Colonialism lost most of its ground in the late twentieth century. However, neocolonialism continues—the indirect ways nations or other groups try to dominate other peoples.

4. P. Christopher Earley of London Business School and Ang Soon of Nanyang Technical University in Singapore have led the charge on constructing the theory and related research regarding CQ. I'm indebted to Soon in particular, a fellow follower of Christ, who has encouraged me and helped me to adapt this work to missions (see P. Christopher Earley and Ang Soon, *Cultural Intelligence: Individual Interactions across Cultures* [Stanford, CA: Stanford University Press, 2003], 239).

Chapter 1: One World

1. US Census Bureau, "World POPClock Projection," June 17, 2005, www.census.gov/ipc/www/popclockworld.html.

2. Anthony Marsella, "Conflict, Negotiation, and Mediation across Cultures" (lecture, Fourth Biennial Conference on Intercultural Research, Kent, OH, May 5, 2005).

3. Timothy Garton Ash, *Free World: America, Europe, and the Surprising Future of the West* (New York: Random House, 2002), 149.

4. Tim Dearborn, "A Global Future for Local Churches," in *The Local Church in a Global Era: Reflections for a New Century*, ed. M. L. Stackhouse, T. Dearborn, and S. Paeth (Grand Rapids: Eerdmans), 212.

5. Richard Dooling, *White Man's Grave* (New York: Picador, 1994), 168.

6. Many of the statistics in this section come from Bryant L. Myers, *Exploring World Mission: Context and Challenges* (Federal Way, WA: World Vision International, 2003).

7. Bruce Huseby, "AIDS/Razor Blades," email message to author, June 18, 2005.

8. United Nations AIDS Report, "Report on the Global AIDS Epidemic" (New York: United Nations, 2004).

9. United States Committee for Refugees, "World Refugee Survey: Refugee and IDP Statistics" (Washington, DC: USCRI, 2004).

10. Bryant L. Myers, "Compassion with an Attitude: A Humanitarian's View of Human Suffering," *Brandywine Review of Faith and International Affairs* 2, no. 3 (Winter 2004–2005): 51–55.

11. Don Golden, "Sierra Leone Refugee," email message to author, March 20, 2002.

12. Ted Fishman, *China Inc.: How the Rise of the Next Superpower Challenges America and the World* (New York: Scribner, 2005), 343.

13. Shawn Tully, "Teens: The Most Global Market of All," *Fortune*, May 16, 1994, 90.

14. Benjamin Barber, *Jihad vs. McWorld: How Globalism and Tribalism Are Reshaping the World* (New York: Ballantine Books, 1996), 9.

15. Lamin Sanneh and Joel Carpenter, eds., *The Changing Face of Christianity: Africa, the West, and the World* (New York: Oxford University Press, 2005), 222.

Chapter 2: One Church

1. Philip Jenkins, *The Next Christendom: The Coming of Global Christianity* (New York: Oxford University Press, 2002), 2.

2. Ibid., 37.

3. I'm on a campaign to eliminate "third world" from our vocabulary altogether. I'm well aware that it's still used broadly by the media and by many ministry leaders. While the etymology of "third world" is not originally negative (first world being the Allied nations who opposed communism, second world being communist nations, and third world being a third alternative to either capitalism or communism), many people outside the "first" world find the term offensive. "Developed" and "developing" world is better but still connotes that one is ahead of the other. Majority world, a term describing where most of the people in the world live, is the preferred term by nationals in these regions.

4. Sanneh and Carpenter, *Changing Face of Christianity*, 3.

5. David Barrett and Todd Johnson, eds., *World Christian Trends: AD 30–AD 2200* (Pasadena, CA: William Carey Library, 2001), 3–9.

6. Ibid., 4.

7. Sanneh and Carpenter, *Changing Face of Christianity*, 5.

8. Nina Shea, *In the Lion's Den: A Shocking Account of Persecution and Martyrdom of Christians Today and How We Should Respond* (Nashville: Broadman & Holman, 1997), ix.

9. Jenkins, *Next Christendom*, 76.

10. R. Pierce Beaver, "The History of Mission Strategy," in *Perspectives on the World Christian Movement: A Reader,* ed. R. Winter and S. Hawthorne (Pasadena, CA: William Carey Library, 1999), 74.

11. Isaac M. T. Mwase, "Shall They Till with Their Own Hoes? Baptists in Zimbabwe and New Patterns of Interdependence, 1950–2000," in Sanneh and Carpenter, *Changing Face of Christianity,* 74.

12. Sanneh and Carpenter, *Changing Face of Christianity,* 7.

13. Clinton Arnold, *Powers of Darkness: Principalities and Powers in Paul's Letters* (Downers Grove, IL: InterVarsity), 210.

14. Jenkins, *Next Christendom,* 125.

15. Brother Yun and Paul Hattaway, *The Heavenly Man: The Remarkable Story of Chinese Christian Brother Yun* (Grand Rapids: Monarch, 2003), 65.

16. Paul Hattaway, *Back to Jerusalem: Three Chinese House Church Leaders Share Their Vision to Complete the Great Commission* (Waynesboro, GA: Authentic Media, 2003).

17. Sam George, "The Nation with the Most Missionaries Is India," *Friday Fax,* November 5, 2004.

18. World Evangelical Alliance, "Report on Global Consultation on Evangelical Missiology" (lecture, Global Consultation on Evangelical Missiology, Iguacu, Parana, Brazil, October 1999).

19. Hattaway, *Back to Jerusalem,* xi.

Part 2: Conflicting Images

1. Christian Smith, *Soul Searching: The Religious and Spiritual Lives of American Teenagers* (New York: Oxford University Press, 2005), 69.

2. Organizations use different distinctions to define short-term versus long-term missions. For the most part, long-term missions refers to someone who is going for two years or more to live in another culture and do missions. While short-term missions often includes anything less than two years, this book focuses primarily on short-term missions efforts that last ten days to two weeks.

3. The findings shared in this book from my own research have come from a qualitative method using a grounded-theory approach. Data was collected and analyzed through pre-trip and post-trip interviews and journals of North American participants. In addition, the nationals who received the short-term groups were interviewed and completed surveys. Any quotations by short-term participants or nationals without a footnote are from data I've collected. The complete report on the study examining American pastors' training efforts overseas is reported in David Livermore, "The Emperor's New Clothes: Experiences of Stateside Church Leaders Who Train Cross-Culturally" (PhD diss., Michigan State University, 2001).

Chapter 3: Motivation

1. Bulletin announcement, in Glenn Schwartz, "Two Awesome Problems: How Short-Term Missions Can Go Wrong," *International Journal of Frontier Missions* 20, no. 4 (2004): 33.

2. Adapted from Hattaway, *Back to Jerusalem,* 101.

3. The effect our expectations have on how we experience new situations is referred to as "anticipatory socialization." Robert Merton, who initially articulated this theory,

examined how the expectations of US Army recruits influenced their experiences as privates. Merton found that those privates who most accurately anticipated and embraced the US Army culture and its values were the privates most likely to experience promotions within the army's hierarchy. I've done some work applying this important theory to the effect short-termers' expectations had on their actual engagement in short-term missions (see Robert Merton, *Social Theory and Social Structure* [New York: Free Press, 1968], 319).

4. Roger Peterson, Gordon Aeschliman, and R. Wayne Sneed, *Maximum Impact, Short-Term Mission: The God-Commanded Repetitive Deployment of Swift, Temporary Nonprofessional Missionaries* (Minneapolis: STEM, 2003), 199–210.

5. Byron Shearer, "Mission Trip: A Microcosm of Life," *Vision for Youth Magazine*, Spring 2005, 17, 30.

6. *Group Magazine*, November/December 2004, 39.

7. Schwartz, "Two Awesome Problems," 33.

8. Hattaway, *Back to Jerusalem*, 101.

9. R. Judd, "Do Short-Term Programmes Achieve the Purposes for Which They Were Established?" (PhD diss., London Bible College, 1996), 16, 19; Terence Linhart, "The Curricular Nature of Youth Group Short-Term Cross-Cultural Service Projects" (PhD diss., Purdue University, 2004).

10. Terence Linhart, "They Were So Alive: The Spectacle Self and Youth Group Short-Term Mission Trips" (paper presented at the North Central Evangelical Missiological Society Meeting, Deerfield, IL, April 9, 2005).

11. Christian Smith, *Soul Searching: The Religious and Spiritual Lives of American Teenagers* (New York: Oxford University Press, 2005), 69.

12. Ridge Burns and Noel Bechetti, *The Complete Student Missions Handbook* (Grand Rapids: Zondervan, 1990).

13. Marshall Allen, "International Short-Term Missions: A Divergence from the Great Commission?" *Youthworker Journal* 16 (May/June 2001): 41.

14. Ibid.

15. Linhart, "Curricular Nature"; Kurt VerBeek, "The Impact of Short-Term Missions. A Case Study: House Construction in Honduras after Hurricane Mitch," May 3, 2005, www.calvin.edu/academic/sociology/staff/kurt.htm.

16. David Maclure, "Wholly Available? Missionary Motivation where Consumer Choice Reigns," William Carey, 2001, www.williamcarey.org.uk/FILES/essay1.htm.

17. Jeff Edmondson, "The End of the Youth Mission Trip as We Know It," *Youthworker Journal* 16 (May/June 2001): 30–34.

18. Reported from a fellow missionary to JoAnn Van Engen, "The Cost of Short-Term Missions," *The Other Side* (January/February 2000): 20.

19. VerBeek, "Impact of Short-Term Missions."

Chapter 4: Urgency

1. Dooling, *White Man's Grave* (New York: Picador, 1994), 146.

2. Robert Webber, *The Younger Evangelicals: Facing the Challenges of the New World* (Grand Rapids: Baker, 2002), 41.

3. Roger Peterson, Gordon Aeschliman, and R. Wayne Sneed, *Maximum Impact, Short-Term Mission: The God-Commanded Repetitive Deployment of Swift, Temporary Nonprofessional Missionaries* (Minneapolis: STEM, 2003), 29.

4. Rob Bell, "Jesus Is Difficult," part 3 (sermon, Mars Hill Bible Church, Grandville, MI, April 17, 2005).

Chapter 5: Common Ground

1. Earley and Soon, *Cultural Intelligence*, 239.

2. Paul H. Ray and Sherry Ruth Anderson, *The Cultural Creatives: How Fifty Million People Are Changing the World* (New York: Three Rivers, 2001), 41.

3. Terence Linhart, "They Were So Alive: The Spectacle Self and Youth Group Short-Term Mission Trips" (paper presented at the North Central Evangelical Missiological Society Meeting, Deerfield, IL, April 9, 2005), 7.

4. Ibid.

5. Stuart Hall, *Representation: Cultural Representation and Signifying Practices* (Thousand Oaks, CA: SAGE, 1997).

Chapter 6: The Bible

1. Jacob Loewen, "The Gospel: Its Content and Communication," in *Down to Earth: Studies in Christianity and Culture,* ed. J. Stott and R. Coote (Grand Rapids: Eerdmans, 1980), 121.

2. I explore this further in my book *Connecting Your Journey with the Story of God: Disciplemaking in Diverse Contexts* (Elburn, IL: Sonlife Ministries, 2001).

3. Michael Horton, ed., *A Confessing Theology for Postmodern Times* (Wheaton: Crossway, 2001), 96.

4. Ibid., 99.

5. N. T. Wright, *The Challenge of Jesus: Rediscovering Who Jesus Was and Is* (Downers Grove, IL: InterVarsity, 1999), 181.

6. I discuss this further in my book *Connecting Your Journey with the Story of God.*

7. Arthur Patzia, *The Emergence of the Church: Context, Growth, Leadership, and Worship* (Downers Grove, IL: InterVarsity, 2001), 13.

8. My GRTS colleague Gary Meadors provides some helpful perspective and tools for applying Scripture to our current contexts in his book *Decision Making God's Way* (Grand Rapids: Baker, 2003), 104–26.

9. Aida Besancon Spencer and William David Spencer, eds., *The Global God: Multicultural Evangelical Views of God* (Grand Rapids: Baker, 1998).

10. Mark Noll, back cover of *The Global God.*

Chapter 7: Money

1. Brad Pitt, interview by Diane Sawyer, *Primetime Live*, ABC News, June 7, 2005.

2. Ibid.

3. Simon Robinson, "Do They Know It's Simplistic? Band-Aid's Intentions Are Good but Africa Needs More than Just a Christmas Jingle," *Time*, November 28, 2004, www.time.com/time/europe/.

4. Glenn Schwartz, "Two Awesome Problems: How Short-Term Missions Can Go Wrong," *International Journal of Frontier Missions* 20, no. 4 (2004): 32.

5. Jo Ann Van Engen, "The Cost of Short-Term Missions," *The Other Side* (January/February 2000): 21.

6. Ibid., 22.

7. Schwartz, "Two Awesome Problems," 28.

8. Shane Claiborne, "Downward Mobility in an Upscale World," *The Other Side* (November/December 2000), 11.

9. Dooling, *White Man's Grave*, 157.

10. Max Van Manen, "Moral Language and Pedagogical Experience," *Journal of Curriculum Studies* 32, no. 2 (March/April 2000): 315–27.

11. Terence Linhart, "They Were So Alive: The Spectacle Self and Youth Group Short-Term Mission Trips" (paper presented at the North Central Evangelical Missiological Society Meeting, Deerfield, IL, April 9, 2005), 6.

12. Ibid., 9.

13. Van Engen, "Cost of Short-Term Missions," 22.

Chapter 8: Simplicity

1. President George W. Bush, transcript of address to joint session of congress, CNN, September 20, 2001, http://archives.cnn.com/2001/US/09/20/gen.bush.transcript/.

2. Jefferson Morley, "Michael Moore, Ugly American: Filmmaker Taken to Task for Arrogance, Ignoring Israel," *Washington Post*, July 13, 2004.

3. Linhart, "They Were So Alive," 6.

4. Ibid., 10.

5. R. Slimbach, "First, Do No Harm: Short-Term Missions at the Dawn of a New Millennium," *Evangelical Missions Quarterly* 36, no. 4 (October 2000): 432.

6. Terence Linhart, "The Curricular Nature of Youth Group Short-Term Cross-Cultural Service Projects" (PhD diss., Purdue University, 2004), 190–91.

Part 3: Sharpening Our Focus and Service with Cultural Intelligence (CQ)

1. P. Christopher Earley of London Business School and Ang Soon of Naynang Business School in Singapore developed CQ as a framework for nurturing effective cross-cultural interactions. The focus of their work has been the cross-cultural interactions of those in the business world and the hospitality industry. I've had the privilege of interacting with Ang Soon a number of times and am grateful for her help in adapting CQ for use in the missions arena. See Earley and Soon, *Cultural Intelligence*.

2. The case study of college students traveling to Shanghai is fictitious, though it was developed using my research on short-term experiences.

Chapter 9: Try, Try Again

1. Earley and Soon, *Cultural Intelligence*, 124.

2. When we do this, we engage in what marriage counselors call "idealistic distortion"—the tendency to see something in an overly positive manner and to believe that rose-colored view is reality. Sometimes marriages are eroding, but the husband is in such denial that he sees the marriage as he longs for it to be, even though that isn't close to reality. We often do this with our short-term missions experiences.

Chapter 10: Seek to Understand

1. A portion of this material was adapted from Kenneth Cushner and R. W. Brislin, *Intercultural Interactions: A Practical Guide* (Thousand Oaks, CA: SAGE, 1996).

2. Geert Hofstede, *Cultures and Organizations: Software of the Mind* (New York: McGraw-Hill, 1997), 5.

3. Robert Levine, *A Geography of Time: The Temporal Misadventures of a Social Psychologist, or How Every Culture Keeps Time Just a Little Bit Differently* (New York: Basic, 1997).

4. P. Christopher Earley, Ang Soon, and Tan Joo-Seng, *CQ: Cultural Intelligence at Work* (Stanford, CA: Stanford University Press, 2006).

5. Edward Hall and M. R. Hall, *Understanding Cultural Differences: Germans, French, and Americans* (Yarmouth, ME: Intercultural, 1990).

6. Hofstede explored five dimensions that help expose cultural differences: individualism, power distance, uncertainty avoidance, masculinity, and long-term orientation. The first three are the most useful for developing CQ Knowledge (see Geert Hofstede, *Culture's Consequences: International Differences in Work-Related Values* [Newbury Park, CA: SAGE, 1980]).

7. L. Robert Kohls and John Knight, *Developing Intercultural Awareness: A Cross-Cultural Training Handbook* (Yarmouth, ME: Intercultural, 1994), 44.

8. Ibid., 45.

9. Riki Takeuchi, Paul Tesluk, and Sophia Marinova, "Role of International Experiences in the Development of Cultural Intelligence" (paper presented at the Academy of Management, New Orleans, LA, August 11, 2004).

10. Adapted from Hall and Hall, *Understanding Cultural Differences*; Levine, *Geography of Time*; and Hofstede, *Culture's Consequences*.

11. David Thomas and Kerr Inkson, *Cultural Intelligence: People Skills for Global Business* (San Francisco: Berrett-Koehler, 2004), 19.

Chapter 11: On Second Thought

1. Ang Soon, personal communication with the author, April 22, 2005.

2. David Thomas and Kerr Inkson, *Cultural Intelligence: People Skills for Global Business* (San Francisco: Berrett-Koehler, 2004), 52.

3. Adapted from Keith Ferrazzi's use of the Johari window in his business book on networking (see Keith Ferrazzi, *Never Eat Alone: And Other Secrets to Success, One Relationship at a Time* [New York: Random House, 2005], 154).

4. Riki Takeuchi, Paul Tesluk, and Sophia Marinova, "Role of International Experiences in the Development of Cultural Intelligence" (paper presented at the Academy of Management, New Orleans, LA, August 11, 2004).

5. Kenneth Cushner, *Beyond Tourism: A Practical Guide to Meaningful Educational Travel* (Lanham, MD: Scarecrow Educational, 2004), 45.

Chapter 12: Actions Speak Louder than Words

1. Earley and Soon, *Cultural Intelligence*, 5.

Chapter 13: The Heart of the Matter

1. N. T. Wright, *Following Jesus: Biblical Reflections on Discipleship* (Grand Rapids: Eerdmans, 1994), 10.

2. David Livermore and Steve Argue, *Explore 1: Shepherd through Following* (Grand Rapids: Intersect, 2005), 6–7.

3. Kenda Creasy Dean, *Practicing Passion: Youth and the Quest for a Passionate Church* (Grand Rapids: Eerdmans, 2004), 192–93.

4. Henri Nouwen, *In the Name of Jesus: Reflections on Christian Leadership* (New York: Crossroad, 1989).

5. Jonathan Edwards, "Thoughts on the Revival of Religion in New England," in *The Works of Jonathan Edwards*, vol. 1 (Carlisle, PA: Banner of Truth Trust, 1834), 380.

6. Chip Huber, "Building a Community Bridge across the World: The God-Engineered Link between Chicago and Zambia," *Youthworker Journal* 20, no. 4 (July/August 2005): 46–49.

7. Leslie Newbigin, *The Open Secret: An Introduction to the Theology of Mission* (Grand Rapids: Eerdmans, 1995), 174.

8. David Stoner, "The Missional Church Is Passionately 'Glocal': A North American Perspective," *Connections*, March 2005.

David A. Livermore (PhD, Michigan State University) is president of the Cultural Intelligence Center in East Lansing, Michigan, and has written several books on cultural intelligence and global leadership. He has worked with leaders in more than one hundred countries globally.

www.davidlivermore.com.

Also by David Livermore

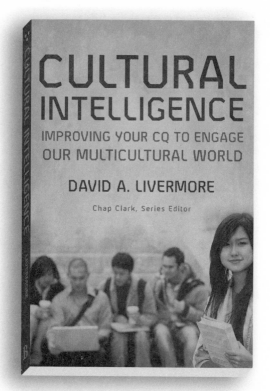

Cultural Intelligence
IMPROVING YOUR CQ TO ENGAGE OUR MULTICULTURAL WORLD
by Dave Livermore
9780801035890   288 pp.

Twenty-first-century society is diverse, and Christians must be able to understand other cultures and communicate effectively between and among them. This new addition to the Youth, Family, and Culture series explores the much-needed skill of Cultural Intelligence (CQ), the ability to work effectively across national, ethnic, and even organizational cultures.

While rooted in sound, scholarly research, *Cultural Intelligence* is highly practical and accessible to general readers. It will benefit students as well as guide ministry leaders interested in increasing their cultural awareness and sensitivity. Packed with assessment tools, simulations, case studies, and exercises, *Cultural Intelligence* will help transform individuals and organizations into effective intercultural communicators of the gospel.

Baker Academic
a division of Baker Publishing Group
www.BakerAcademic.com